*U*nderstanding
*C*olor

Understanding Color

An Introduction for Designers

LINDA HOLTZSCHUE

 VAN NOSTRAND REINHOLD
I(T)P A Division of International Thomson Publishing Inc.

New York • Albany • Bonn • Boston • Detroit • London • Madrid • Melbourne
Mexico City • Paris • San Francisco • Singapore • Tokyo • Toronto

I(T)P™ A division of International Thomson Publishing, Inc.
        The ITP logo is a trademark under license

Printed in the United States of America

For more information, contact:

Van Nostrand Reinhold   Chapman & Hall GmbH
115 Fifth Avenue   Pappelallee 3
New York, NY 10003   69469 Weinheim
                                         Germany

Chapman & Hall   International Thomson Publishing Asia
2-6 Boundary Row   221 Henderson Road #05-10
London   Henderson Building
SE1 8HN   Singapore 0315
United Kingdom

Thomas Nelson Australia   International Thomson Publishing Japan
102 Dodds Street   Hirakawacho Kyowa Building, 3F
South Melbourne, 3205   2-2-1 Hirakawacho
Victoria, Australia   Chiyoda-ku, 102 Tokyo
                                         Japan

Nelson Canada   International Thomson Editores
1120 Birchmount Road   Campos Eliseos 385, Piso 7
Scarborough, Ontario   Col. Polanco
Canada M1K 5G4   11560 Mexico D.F. Mexico

4 5 6 7 8 9 10 COR-WF 01 00 99 98 97

Library of Congress Cataloging-in-Publication Data

Holtzschue, Linda.
    Understanding color : an introduction for designers / Linda
    Holtzschue
        p.   cm.
    Includes bibliographical references and index.
    ISBN 0-442-01683-2
    1. Color in design.   I. Titles
NK1548.H66 1994   94-7910
701'.82—dc20   CIP

Dedication

To my children Alison, Adam, and Sara for their endless patience, to my mother for her gifts of confidence and love, to the memory of my father whose vitality and inspiration I miss every day, and to my sisters and my friends for their cheerful and unwavering support. Most of all to Karl, whose unconditional love and encouragement made it possible.

Contents

6 Using Color 73

Preface

A poor product, colored well, will often sell. A great product, poorly colored, will not move from the shelves.

This is a book for everyone who uses color. It was written for design students and sign painters, architects and carpet salespeople, graphic artists and magicians. It's a road map through the mysteries of color and a guide to using color freely, comfortably, and creatively without dependence on complicated theories or systems. This is a book about learning to see.

Acknowledgments

My thanks to Mike O'Connell and Joann Preston for their contributions to the illustrations, and to Ed Goldberg and Jack Fields of Edward Fields Carpets, Mrs. Murray Douglas of Brunschwig and Fils, Nancy Picunko of Sanderson, Jay Pomeroy of General Electric, Richard O'Brien of Color Aid Corp., and Pantone, Inc. for their generous contributions of material for illustration purposes. Many thanks to Dr. Ivan Bodis-Wollner of Rockefeller University for sharing with me the lecture material on Newton and Goethe, and to old friends John Stevenson, Ph.D., for his material on Newton and the controversies of the eighteenth century, and Leonard Shaw, Ph.D., for his review of the chapter on light and color. The help I received from Doug Wise in understanding the capabilities of computers and color was invaluable.

C h a p t e r 1

A Little Light on the Subject

Yesterday upon the stair
I met a man who wasn't there
He wasn't there again today
I wish to heck he'd go away.

(ANONYMOUS)

The most surprising and interesting thing about color is that just like the man upon the stair, it's not really "there." Color isn't real in the sense of having substance or body. It can't be touched or shaped. Of course, a colored *object* can be touched and shaped, but it's the object itself that has substance, not its color. Color is only appearance; something seen at a given moment and nothing more.

Compounding this elusive nature of color, the same object often appears to be a completely different color when it's moved from one location to another. Everyone has experienced painting a wall and being astonished at the resulting color, or buying an article of clothing and arriving home to find that it's a mysteriously different color than it was in the store. Color is no more permanent or absolute than the place and the light in which we see it.

The instability of color arises from two very different causes. The first is based in science; how color is generated by light and seen by the human eye.[1]

Any science requires measurable elements or responses. The chemistry of colorants (dyes and pigments), the physics of light, human visual acuity, and psychology are measurable. The color of an object will seem to change in time and place because there are three variable factors in the perception of color:

> the light source
>
> the object
>
> the viewer

These three variables interact so closely that if any one changes, the color of the same object may appear to change.

The Light Source

The first part of the light/object/viewer equation is light. Only light generates color. Without light, no color exists. The sly old metaphor has a literal meaning; all cats really are gray in the dark.

. . . .

[1]The second cause of apparent change in colors is a consequence of the placement of colors relative to one another. Placement can be accidental or deliberate, inadvertent or part of the creative process. Color change by placement is covered in Chapter 6, Using Color.

Light is visible energy. The human eye is a sensor adapted to "receive" light. The retina of the eye receives the energy signal and transmits it to the brain, which "names" the color. A light source emits this visible energy in waves. A light source can be any one of a number of things; the sun, a luminous panel, a light bulb. All light travels at the same speed, but the pulses of light energy may be emitted at different distances apart (or frequencies). The distance between these peaks or waves of energy emission is called *wavelength*. Wavelengths of light are measured in nanometers (nm).

The human eye is able to perceive wavelengths of light ranging from about 380 to 720 nm. The full range of visible light is the visible spectrum. Certain wavelengths are perceived as separate colors; from red, the longest visible wavelength (720 nm), through orange, yellow, green, blue, and indigo (blue-violet) to violet, the shortest visible wavelength (380 nm). An acronym for the visible wavelengths is "ROYG-BIV" (**R**ed/**O**range/**Y**ellow/**G**reen/**B**lue/**I**ndigo/**V**iolet).[2] (See Figure C–2 in color insert.)

There is visible light beyond the range of human vision. Many insects can detect ultraviolet, a shorter wavelength beyond violet. Both ultraviolet and infrared (the longer wavelength beyond red) can be made visible to the human eye with special optical equipment.

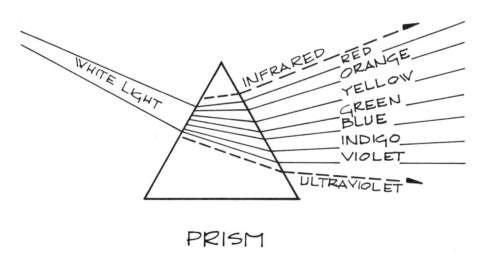

PRISM

Figure 1–1 *The Component Wavelengths of White Light.* The individual wavelengths (colors) that make up white light can be seen by passing the light through a prism. The prism bends each wavelength at a slightly different angle so that each emerges as a separate beam.

. . . .

[2]The individual wavelengths of light can be seen when white light is passed through a prism. The prism refracts (bends) the various wavelengths at slightly different angles so that each emerges as a separate beam.

The perception of color involving only the viewer and a light source is called the *illuminant mode of vision*. In the illuminant mode of vision, there is no object, only the light source and the eye. Television and computer screens, traffic lights, and neon signs are familiar experiences of the illuminant mode of vision, color seen as light only. [3]

Mixing Light: Additive Color

When separate wavelengths (colors) of light are combined, the outcome seems illogical to nonscientists. For light to appear as white (or colorless) it must contain the three primary colors of light—the red, green, and blue wavelengths. If even one of the light primaries is absent, the light will not be white. (See Figure C–4).

The red and green wavelengths combined (added together) yield yellow light. The blue and green wavelengths added together make cyan (blue-green) light, and the blue and red wavelengths make magenta (red-violet). Yellow, cyan, and magenta are the secondary colors of light. [4]

White or colored light seen as a result of a combination of wavelengths is called an *additive mixture*. The term is a good description of the reality because additive mixtures occur as wavelengths are added to

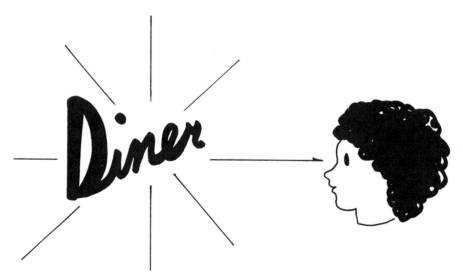

Figure 1–2 *Additive Color.* A neon sign is a familiar form of light seen as color. Neon signs are lamps that emit a limited range of wavelengths (colors).

. . . .

[3] See "Computers and Color" on page 17.

[4] Any two or three secondary colors of light added together will also produce white light because they already include the three primaries.

each other.[5] Additive mixtures (colors of light) occur only in the illuminant mode of vision.

Lamps

The sun is our fundamental light source. Light bulbs are the next most universal source of light. There are hundreds of different types of light bulbs. The correct term for a light bulb is a *lamp*. The fixture that holds the lamp is a luminaire. What we commonly call a lamp is technically a "portable luminaire." The most familiar lamps are the "A-lamp," or ordinary incandescent light bulb, and the fluorescent tube.

If a lamp emits light of only one or a few wavelengths, that light is seen as a single color. Neon lamps are an example of light emission in only one or a few wavelengths. Another source may emit light in a broader, but still limited range of wavelengths, and that light too will be seen as color. Sodium lamps, often used on expressways and in parking lots, emit light almost entirely from the red/orange/yellow range. Most lamps produce white light because, like the sun, they emit all of the visible wavelengths. A catchall phrase for lamps that emit white light is "general light source."

Each type of lamp emits the various wavelengths in a characteristic pattern called a *spectral reflectance curve* (or spectral distribution curve). A lamp may give off all or most of the wavelengths, but each will be given off at a different relative strength or quantity. If the wavelengths leaving the lamp were colored ribbons, some ribbons would be thicker, wider, and stronger than the other ribbons. (See Figure C–2.)

The spectral reflectance curve provides a visual profile of the color characteristics of any light source. It shows the strengths of the various wavelengths relative to each other for that particular type of lamp. Every lamp is described technically in this way. Spectral reflectance makes it easy to compare the color quality of two or more light sources, whether the white light has a "warm" (yellow or red) or "cool" (green or blue) cast.

The quantity of light emitted by a lamp is unrelated to its spectral distribution. The same lamp type may give off more or less light (a 250 watt incandescent lamp versus a 75 watt, for example), but the spectral reflectance curve or pattern of relative energy emitted at the different wavelengths will be identical for that lamp type no matter what the wattage.[6]

. . . .

[5]To lighting designers, the word "chromaticity" means the relative whiteness of a light source. Other designers and artists use the word "chroma" or "chromatic" to mean the presence of color.

[6]Although quantity of light emitted by any lamp is not a concern in lamp color, amount of light emitted does affect the viewer's ability to see colors of objects. See "Adaptation" in Chapter 2.

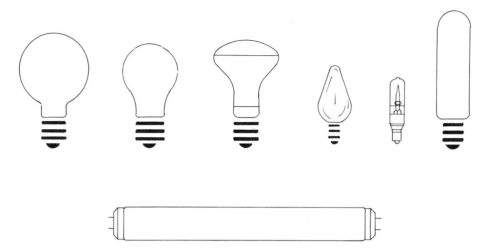

Figure 1–3 *Lamps.* Lamps are available in hundreds of shapes and sizes. In addition to differences in size and shape, each has its own characteristic pattern of spectral reflectance.

The presence of most or all visible wavelengths in a light source (as long as the red, green, and blue are included) will always yield white light. Because of differences in spectral distribution, lamps yielding white light do so in different ways. A typical fluorescent lamp may give off all wavelengths nearly equally, while an incandescent lamp may give off more light in the red/orange/yellow range than in the blue or green range.

The human eye is most sensitive to the yellow-green wavelengths. Maybe this genetic predisposition to green is a response to the needs of food gathering—to finding the freshest green vegetation. Whatever the reason, given the same energy output at each wavelength, the eye will sense yellow-green as the brightest and red and blue as the darkest.

Because of the eye's sensitivity to yellow-green, a fluorescent lamp emitting the visible wavelengths at roughly equal levels will appear white, but greenish-white. Incandescent lamps are stronger in the yellow-red ranges and the light they emit will appear more yellow-orange white. The spectral reflectance curve determines the visual quality of a light source, its warmth, coolness, or neutral whiteness.

Most lamps are described and marketed as being more or less similar in spectral reflectance to sunlight. Manufacturers sometimes market lamps as "full-spectrum" which is truthful but gives the misleading impression that the light will be "true," or close to daylight.

To refer to a light source as "true," or even as "natural" or "artificial," is deceptive. It leads to the misconception that there is "true" light and as a corollary its opposite, "false" light. We think of "natural" (sunlight or daylight) and "artificial" (any other) light as if they were different entities, but no source produces light that is more natural than another. Light is simply light; it is visible energy. What we can say is that there are naturally occurring light sources and man-made ones and that daylight is a convenient standard for comparison.

Lamp Color, Human Comfort, and Performance

The ability to see to perform most tasks is the ability to see the difference between dark and light, not the ability to detect color. Black and white photographs and movies are perfectly understandable. Color-blind individuals may function very well. The ability to see dark/light contrast is unaffected by lamp color. Only lighting level, the quantity of available light, affects the ability to see dark and light differences. And although many people report different levels of comfort under a variety of light sources, human performance under general light sources has not been shown to be affected by lamp color, only by lighting levels. (*General Electric Lighting Application Bulletin #205–41311*).[7]

The Object Mode of Vision

Color problems in the design industries rarely involve additive mixtures or the illuminant mode of vision. The colors of objects—raw materials and finished products, media, textiles, printed materials, and anything else that has color—are the everyday concern of the design professional.

The impact of light seen as color is very different from the impact of the color of objects. A classic misunderstanding of that difference took place when fire engines were for a brief period painted yellow-green for high visibility instead of the traditional red. The reason given was that the sensitivity of the eye to the yellow-green range of light made yellow-green the most visible and therefore the safest color. Fire engines are objects, not wavelengths of light. Very different principles of high visibility apply. Yellow-green fire engines disappeared very quickly and the traditional red returned, an outcome not of nostalgia but of practical reality. Red fire engines are more visible in the landscape than yellow-green ones.[8]

In the illuminant mode of vision, the viewer sees light as color. In the *object mode of vision,* the viewer sees color in tangible objects. The object mode of vision has three variables: light source, object, and viewer. Objects and their colorants are materials. In the object mode of vision, light is modified by materials. Materials modify light in one of the following three ways:

Transmission: The light passes through a material, as through glass.

Absorption: The material soaks up the light like a sponge, so it is lost as visible light.

Scattering or reflection: The light is neither passed through nor absorbed. It bounces off the object, changing direction and scattering.

. . . .

[7]As a rule of thumb, the "better" (warmer, more pleasing, and less green) the light source, the lower the efficiency of the lamp.

[8]See Chapter 7, Color Harmony/Color Effect.

Light leaving the light source is called the *incident beam*. When the incident beam reaches an object or surface, some or all of the light is reflected back to the eye. That light is the *reflected* beam.

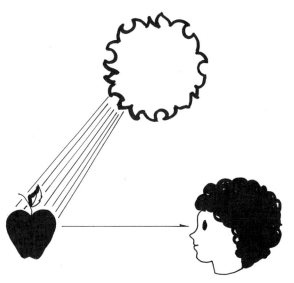

Figure 1–4 *The Object Mode of Vision.* Wavelengths (colors) of light from a general source are both absorbed and reflected by an object. The absorbed wavelengths are lost as visible. The reflected wavelengths bounce off the object and reach the viewer, who sees the object as that color.

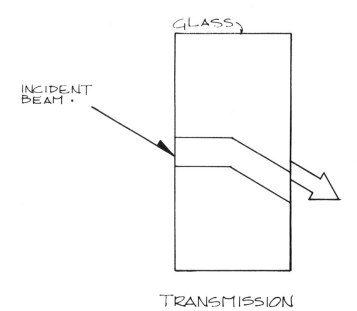

Figure 1–5 *Transmission.* White light is transmitted or passes through window glass with no perceptible loss. Unlike the thick glass of a prism, thin glass bends the light so slightly that it retains its identity as white light.

Surfaces, Smooth and Rough

When a surface is smooth the reflection or scattering is very direct; a good deal of light reaches the eye. When a surface is rough, even microscopically rough, light is scattered in more directions and the surface appears both softer and darker. A surface that is minutely roughened, diffusing and spreading light, has a *matte* finish. Polished or smooth surfaces that reflect light more directly and sharply have a *gloss* or *glossy* finish.

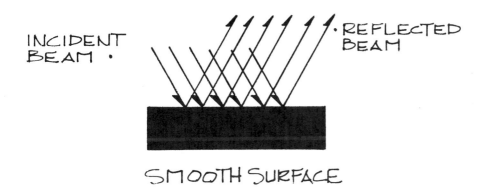

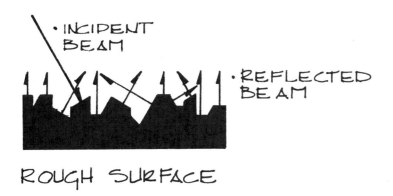

Figure 1–6 *Surfaces and Light Reflection.* Smooth and rough surfaces reflect light differently. Light reaching a smooth surface is reflected very directly off the surface. Light reaching a rough surface is reflected in many more different directions and the surface appears darker.

A specular surface is so reflective that much of the light reaching it from a general source returns to the eye directly (as white light) before it gets to the underlying colorant. Materials or objects with gloss or specular surfaces are very reflective of white light, but the underlying colorant can actually appear darker than it would if the surface were matte. Much of the light has been reflected off the top surface before reaching the colorant.

The sun is such a powerful source of light energy that to look directly into it will cause permanent damage to the eye. Strong man-made light sources can also cause eye injury if viewed directly. No sensible person looks into a light source deliberately, but too powerful reflected light can also cause discomfort or even eye damage.

Glare is an extreme, physically fatiguing level of reflected light. Very high light levels combined with an extremely reflective surface result in glare. Glare obliterates color perception and is temporarily blinding. In extreme cases like extended exposure to the reflection off snow, glare can cause permanent damage to vision.[9]

Colorants

Colorants (or color agents, dyes, or dyestuff) are the substances or materials that modify light by absorbing some wavelengths of light and reflecting others. A colorant can be applied to the surface of an object, like paint or lacquer, or it may be integrated into the material, as in a dyed textile, a solid plastic, or a stone.

If an object is placed under a general light source (white light) and all of the wavelengths of that light are reflected by its colorant, the object will appear to be white. Under the same light source, if all of the wavelengths of light reaching the object are absorbed by the colorant, the object will appear black. If the object has a colorant that absorbs all of the wavelengths except the red, and reflects the red wavelength only, the object will appear red. If that same object is placed under a light source that lacks the red wavelength, that object will appear black. The red colorant can reflect only the red wavelength. If no red wavelength is present, all light reaching the object will be absorbed and none will be reflected back.

Colorants don't absorb and reflect individual wavelengths perfectly. They may absorb part of a wavelength and reflect two, three, or more wavelengths. There are so many possibilities that the range of visible colors is nearly infinite. Colors seen as the result of the absorption of light are *subtractive mixtures*. Colorants "subtract," or absorb, some wavelengths. The ones that remain are reflected and reach the eye.

. . . .

[9]Indirect lighting will reduce glare. See Chapter 1, "Indirect Light, Indirect Color Below."

Reflectance is the amount of light falling on a surface that is reflected back. Reflectance means the *total* amount of light reflected, not the specific wavelengths (or color). Reflectance is so important to some industries, such as paint and print production products (inks and films), that the percentage of light reflected back is part of the basic information the manufacturer provides about that colorant.

Transparent, Opaque, and Translucent

Some light is always lost when light is transmitted (passes) through a material, but the light loss can be so slight that as a practical matter it's imperceptible. If almost all of the light reaching an object or material is transmitted, that object is transparent. Window glass is an example of transparent material.

If all of the light reaching an object is reflected, the object will appear to be white and opaque. If some wavelengths are absorbed and some reflected, the object will have a color and still appear opaque. If all of the light reaching an object is absorbed and none reflected, the object will be black and opaque.

When some of the light reaching an object or material is transmitted (passed through) and some is reflected, the object is translucent. A translucent material can be white or a color, depending on its selective transmission and reflection of the various wavelengths. It may transmit a great deal of light and be very translucent, or transmit very little light and be barely translucent.

Light Sources and Color Rendition

In order for all possible colors of objects to be seen, the primary colors of light (blue, red, and green wavelengths) must be present in the light source. A light source that lacks one or more of the primaries will render some of the possible colors of objects, but not all of them.

Light sources may contain all the wavelengths but be relatively weak in one or more of them. Because of the great variety in their spectral reflectance, different light sources vary enormously in their color rendition (the ability to reflect colorants). For example, fluorescent lamps are used in grocery stores for their high light output, low heat, and low operating cost. But the low level of red wavelength makes them unsuitable for displaying certain foods. Grocers choose lamps with stronger red wavelengths over meat counters to ensure that the packaged meats appear fresh and red.

Color choices made under one set of light conditions for use in another set of conditions can be a disaster. Every so often an otherwise conventionally dressed woman is seen wearing astonishing bright red makeup. The most likely explanation for the over-coloring is that she applied her cosmetics under fluorescent lighting. Because of the weakness of the red wavelength in fluorescent light, it took enormous quantities of the colorant (her makeup) to reflect any visible red at all under that light. In daylight the red is overwhelming, but if she works under an ambient light source that is also fluorescent, she may never be aware of the garish effect.

In residential interior design considerations of lamp color (and its resulting color rendition) usually take precedence over light output and efficiency. Incandescent lamps are nearly always chosen over fluorescents as a general source. Lamps can be selected for color adjustment or correction in completed interiors. Color selected in daylight may be too warm or too cool for night lighting. Red/orange schemes can be muted by using a lamp with a weaker warm range; color schemes that are too blue or green in night lighting can be warmed up with lamps stronger in the red/orange/yellow range. Manufacturers even recommend specific lamps for different color schemes—one for warm color schemes, another for cool ones.

Lamp choices for commercial applications (including such crucial areas as studio work spaces) are frequently made for light output and energy efficiency without consideration of color rendering qualities, despite the fact that for many products like foods, flowers, cosmetics, and carpets, color rendition is critical.

Comparing Colorants

Colorants, like lamps, can be compared in a laboratory by measuring their spectral reflectance. Lamps are compared by the relative power of emission at each wavelength. Colorants are compared by the reflective power at each wavelength. The spectral reflectance of two or more colorants can be compared only under the same light source. The light source usually used for color comparisons in a laboratory is a Macbeth lamp, which has a spectral reflectance curve similar to sunlight. One color sample is designated as a standard and others are measured against it, under the Macbeth lamp, using a tool called a photocolorimeter.

It's a common misconception that there's a "true" color for every object that can be captured by the correct lamp. A Macbeth lamp is a superb laboratory tool, but it isn't a general light source. The most commonly used lamps are A-lamps (ordinary incandescent light bulbs) and cool fluorescents. Both are quite different in spectral reflectance from the sun or from Macbeth lamps. If ideal, "true" colors existed, and were only visible under Macbeth lamps or outdoors in sunlight, hardly anyone would ever see them.

The ability to measure light reflected from a colorant under controlled laboratory conditions doesn't have much practical application for the artist or designer, but it is enormously useful for quality control in industry.

Luminosity

Luminosity is a commonly used word in color study. Its real meaning is the attribute of emitting light without heat. A luminous object is light reflective but doesn't emit heat. The word luminous is used more commonly to describe light-reflective colors and colorants. For example, watercolor is described as a luminous medium because the light reaching through the colorant to the white of the underlying paper creates the effect of a sparkling, brilliant surface. Watercolor on black paper is dull and dingy because no light is reflected back from the underlying paper.

Indirect Light, Indirect Color

Indirect lighting occurs when light reaches a broad surface that reflects or scatters it onto a second surface or object. This happens when the light source, reflective surface, and an object or space to be lighted are at angles to each other.[10]

Moonlight is the most familiar form of indirect light. The moon is luminous; it reflects light but is not a light source. The moon doesn't emit its own energy. Its surface reflects the light of the sun. Each time light travels, some of that light is lost through scattering. Moonlight is weaker than sunlight because much of the sun's light has been scattered and lost, first on its way from the sun to the moon, then again from the moon to the earth. Still, the moon is an efficient reflector; moonlight can be strong enough to read by.

Indirect lighting works in the same way as moonlight. Indirect lighting has no real impact on color rendition when the intervening reflective surface is white. A general (white) light source directed at a white reflective surface reflects or scatters white light onto a second surface or object. That object may appear slightly darker than it might under a strong, direct light, but no real change in its apparent color takes place. The object appears just as it would if it were directly under a slightly weaker source of light.

Indirect color is another manifestation of indirect lighting. It, too, relies on the placement of a light source, reflective surface, and target object or area. Indirect color occurs when a general light source reaches a highly reflective colorant on a broad plane, and that colorant reflects onto a second object or area. The apparent color of a second object or surface changes. Imagine that a general light source is directed at a broad surface with a very reflective green colorant. The surface absorbs

. . . .

[10]Indirect lighting effects can be modified by changing the angle at which the light source strikes the reflective surfaces. Laws of physics govern these effects.

all wavelengths except the green, which is scattered or reflected onto a nearby chicken. The indirect light (green) reaches the chicken. If the chicken is white, its surface will reflect the green wavelength. The chicken appears to be green. If the chicken has a color of its own, its appearance will depend on that colorant's interaction with the green wavelength reaching it. If, for example, the chicken has red feathers, the green wavelength reflected onto the chicken from the reflective surface will be absorbed. Because it receives little or no red wavelength, the chicken appears dark and dull.[11]

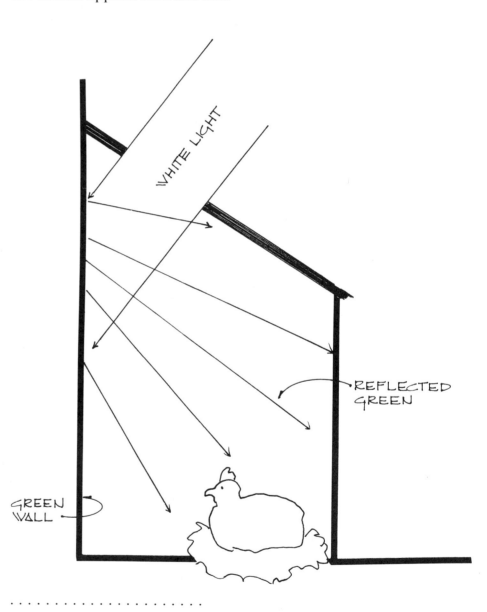

Figure 1–7 *Indirect Color.* The wavelengths of light hitting a green wall in the henhouse are absorbed, but the green wavelength reflected from the paint reaches the white chicken. Because a white surface reflects any wavelength, the green wavelength reaching the chicken is reflected to the viewer's eye. The chicken appears to be green.

[11]In addition to the single or narrow range of wavelengths (colors) reflected by the first surface onto the second one, some scattered light from the original source usually reaches it. The strength of the indirect color will be diluted by the presence of light from a general (white) source.

Another way to describe the phenomenon of color reflected from one surface to another is plane reflection. The design applications most vulnerable to this are architecture and interior design, where flat planes of color on walls, floors, and ceilings and directional light sources are often at opposing angles.

Filters

Filters are materials that transmit (pass through) some wavelengths of light and absorb others. When a filter is placed between a light source and an object it modifies the light that will reach the object. A red filter, for example, absorbs all wavelengths of light except red, which it allows to pass through. If an object in front of the filter has a colorant to reflect that red light, the object will appear red. If the object has a white surface, it will also appear red because a white surface will reflect any wavelength reaching it. If the object has a colorant that reflects green, however, it will appear black or near-black. The filter has transmitted only the red wavelength. No green wavelength reaches the object, so none can be reflected back to the eye.

Filters are like Aladdin's genie. They have plenty of power, but they only follow directions. The directions had better be good ones. The *New York Times* once told the story of a restaurateur who wanted to create a romantic atmosphere by bathing his establishment in warm, rosy light. Instead of using lamps with a strong red wavelength (which would have emphasized red, but allowed all other colors to be seen), he installed red theatrical gels (filters), which blocked all the wavelengths except red.

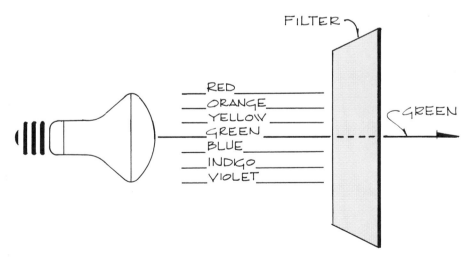

Figure 1–8 *Filters.* A filter selectively absorbs some wavelengths of light and transmits others. When a filter is placed between a light source and an object, only the transmitted wavelengths reach the object.

The gels were extremely effective; vegetables and salads left the kitchen green and arrived at the tables black.

Metamerism and Matching

Materials vary widely in the ways they absorb colorants or accept them as coatings. A substance used as a blue colorant for wool may have little or no relationship to one used to produce blue plastic laminates, blue cotton fibers, blue glass, blue ceramics, or blue woods.

Each colorant, no matter what material it colors, reacts to light in a very specific way. When colorants or substrates (underlying materials) of two objects are different, it's impossible for them to match perfectly under all light conditions. Two objects that appear to match under one set of light conditions but not under another are exhibiting a phenomenon known as *metamerism*. The objects are called a *metameric pair*.

Two red-dyed cottons may appear to match exactly under an incandescent lamp. If their dyes are different, one dye may be more reflective than the other. When the two cottons are placed under a fluorescent lamps which is weaker in the red wavelength, the cotton with the more reflective colorant will appear brighter and "redder" than the other.

"Matching" is usually an aesthetic, production, or marketing issue, not a technical one. "Matching" wallpapers and fabrics, silk shirts and wool skirts, or china sinks and enamelled cast iron bathtubs never truly match because both their underlying materials and colorants are different. What is possible and practical is to reach an acceptable match—one which is pleasing to the eye. When two different materials must reach an acceptable match, the most important thing is to make the comparison under light conditions that duplicate their end placement.

Duplicating the lamp is crucial, but sometimes a choice has to be made between day and night lighting. General Electric suggests that any pair of objects reaching an acceptable match under both fluorescent and incandescent lamps will be acceptable under almost all conditions. (*General Electric Lighting Application Bulletin #205-41311*). This practical advice covers almost all color-compatibility situations as long as the real limitations of color matching between two different materials are understood.[12]

. . . .

[12]In textiles, specific dyes and the fibers that will absorb them are said to have dye affinity. An interesting process illustrates the creative possibilities of dye affinities. Fabric is woven into a pattern using two or more different, undyed fibers. The pattern cannot be seen in the undyed state. The fabric is dipped into successive dye baths, each with an affinity for only one of the fibers. The pattern then becomes visible and many different colorways may be created from the same undyed (or "greige") goods.

The production cost advantages are twofold: many different trial sample colorways can be produced without resetting a loom, and all of the successful colorways can then be woven as running yardage from the same greige goods.

Many manufacturers control acceptable match in related goods by maintaining color laboratories. Sears is known for its care in ensuring that home products (appliances, linens, etc.) are color compatible with each other. A refrigerator purchased in Sears "almond" is very likely to be an acceptable match to Sears "almond" dish towels or pots and both are likely to be pleasing with nationally distributed products (like plastic laminates) with the same color name.

Maintaining a laboratory for color and light problems isn't realistic or necessary for graphic, textile, fashion, or interior designers, architects, small-scale manufacturers, or product designers. The General Electric rule of thumb, "if it's OK under incandescent and fluorescent it's probably OK anywhere," is easy to understand, easy to test, and nearly foolproof.

Exact Matching

A sample submitted for matching is a *standard*. When materials must be dyed, printed, painted, or otherwise matched exactly to a given standard under a variety of lighting conditions, new samples must be made of the identical substrate (material to be colored) and the same colorant used as the original. Perfect under-any-light matching is possible only when the substrates and colorants are identical.

Some manufacturers have the luxury of being able to produce exact matches because they work with a single material and control the complete coloring process. Edward Fields, Inc. manufactures the highest quality wool carpeting. Each new batch of dyes is lab tested for consistency, and every new lot of wool is tested for oil content, which affects readiness to accept dye. Samples and finished product are produced with near-perfect match because substrates and dyes are always the same. In addition, new dyes are constantly being tested to find ways to better resistance to oxidization (fading or color change caused by exposure to light, air, or other environmental factors). After lab testing the components, final samples are dyed and compared to a standard. But at the conclusion of the laboratory testing the final acceptability of the color is judged not by a piece of laboratory equipment but by the dyer—by human eyes alone.

Computers and Color

Computers generate additive mixtures (color as light) as images on a screen. The additive mixtures are programmed to act on screen as if they were subtractive mixtures so that an artist mixing red and green on a computer screen gets what he expects from a paint mixture (a dark "brown") instead of the yellow, which would be the additive result of red and green.

In production of printed material, a computer scanner takes art work (a photographic transparency or piece of opaque art) and, using a

5200° Kelvin lamp, separates the colors into three electrical impulses, one each for cyan, magenta, and yellow. Each impulse is relative in strength to the quantity of that reflected color in the art. The electrical impulses, called analogs, are translated by the scanner into "pixels" (picture elements), which are digital images. The pixels are printed in subtractive colors (using a special medium, process primaries, plus black) directly onto paper.

Computers are wonderful tools. The best computers can produce up to 16 million distinguishable variations of colors. But art work produced with color computers originates in exactly the same way as work produced by hand. Success depends entirely on the artist or designer's ability to use color. Computers enable colorists to try out unlimited numbers of combinations on screen or in print before production of any product, but they cannot think, choose, plan, or design. They are the "fast paint boxes" of design. No computer generates design without human control so computer design remains vulnerable to the fatal disease GIGO (Garbage In, Garbage Out).

References

Lighting Application Bulletin. Undated. General Electric publication #205-41311.

2

The Human Element

Viewer, Visual Acuity and Threshold / Intervals / Naming Colors / The Origins of Confusion: Color Names / Adaptation / Memory Color / Color Constancy

(Sherlock Holmes) "Quite so . . . " he answered, lighting a cigarette and throwing himself down in an armchair, "you see, but you do not observe."

(Dr. Watson) "And yet I believe my eyes are as good as yours."

Sir Arthur Conan Doyle, *"A Scandal in Bohemia"*

In his book *Sensation and Perception,* E. Bruce Goldstein distinguishes between sensation (the actual physical event) and perception (after the sensation, what we believe that we have sensed) (Goldstein 1984). Sensation can be measured in many ways, but perception is a private experience. Only external evidence makes us think that most people see the same thing when they see "red." We accept that something is red, and not blue, not by scientific measurement of wavelengths but by unspoken agreement, common language, and common experience.

The instrument used in solving color problems in the design industries is the normal, unaided human eye.[1] For artists and designers, dyers and house painters, printers and carpet salespeople, even when aided by commercial color charts or professional color sample systems like Color-aid, the Pantone Color Systems, or Plochere, final color choices are made by eye.[2,3] And for each individual, both sensation and perception in response to color are in play at the same time—the ability to detect color differences (visual acuity), which is sensory and physiological, and the idea, concept or inner perception of the experienced color, which is both unconscious (psychological) and conscious (intellectual).[4]

Viewer, Visual Acuity and Threshold

Visual acuity for color is the ability to distinguish between samples. This varies between individuals just as much as the ability to see distance or close detail does. Each person has an individual, self-limiting range of ability to see differences between colors.

. . . .

[1] Clear corrective lenses (untinted eyeglasses or contact lenses) which magnify or correct image distortion are part of normal, unaided color vision. "Color-blindness" is a catchall term for a number of forms of color-deficit vision. A "color-blind" individual may see only dark and light, with no colors at all, or may be deficient in only one or two specific hues.

[2] The Plochere Color System is no longer available to designers but is so well-regarded that it has been preserved in the permanent collection of the Cooper Hewitt Museum of Decorative Arts.

[3] The sensitivity of the human retina to light is very different from the sensitivity of photographic film or technical color measuring instruments used in medicine or industry. Film plays a major role in the reproduction of color and design, but not in the design/color-selection process.

The point at which anyone can just distinguish the difference between two close samples is that individual's threshold. The *threshold* is the measure of visual acuity for color. More precisely, visual acuity for color means the ability to detect differences in hue—between red and orange, for example.

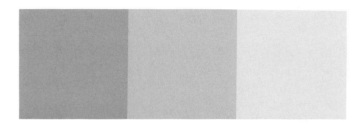

Figure 2–1 *Close Intervals.* For some people intervals this close are the threshold of visual acuity for dark and light. Others with greater visual acuity would be able to see middle steps inserted between them.

An average human eye can see about 150 steps, or different colors, of *light,* whether that color is seen directly from the light source or is reflected from the surface of an object. This number doesn't include darker, lighter, or duller variations of each color. The multiples of the 150 visible colors and their variations mean that an average person can discriminate literally millions of different colors.

The ability to see differences in dark and light is a kind of visual acuity, but it's not really visual acuity for color. Someone who can discriminate very small differences between a darker and lighter gray may not be able to detect a small difference in hue between two similar reds, one of which is slightly more orange or more violet than the other.

Intervals

One way to characterize differences between color samples is in intervals. An *interval* is a visual step between samples. An individual's threshold establishes the single interval, the point at which a detectable middle step can no longer be inserted between two close colors. The *single interval* is specific to each individual—the smallest difference he or she can detect between close samples. Single intervals are important only in determining a person's threshold. In other situations involving intervals there are at least three color samples: the "parents" (samples on

. . . .

[4]Color vision is a complicated and still poorly understood area of physiology. There are two major theories of how color is seen. The trichromatic theory (Young-Von Helmholtz) hypothesizes that color vision results from the stimulation of cones in the eye with different sensitivities to light. The opponent-process theory (Hering) theorizes the buildup and breakdown of a chemical in the retina in response to light.

either side), and the "descendant," a visual step between the two parents.

There are three descriptive qualities of color:

Hue means the name of the color (red, orange, yellow, etc).

Value describes the relative light or dark quality of the sample.

Saturation describes the hue intensity of a color, its dullness or brilliance.

Intervals may be set up between colors having only hue difference, like red and blue; only value difference, like black and white; or only difference in saturation, like brilliant blue and gray-blue. Intervals may also be established between color samples that contrast in two or all qualities. A pale pink and a dark gray-blue have hue, value, and saturation contrast, but a series of intervals may still be set up between them.

Intervals can be broadly spaced with great differences (like black/gray/white) or very close and similar (like red, red/red-orange, and red-orange). In even intervals, the middle sample is visually equidistant between the two parents. For example, a parent-descendant value relationship might be black on one side, white on the other, and gray

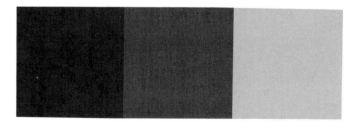

Figure 2–2 *Even and Uneven Intervals.* In the groups of three squares, the end squares are the parents and the center squares are the descendants. In the top figure the descendant gray is closer to its dark parent. In the bottom figure the descendant is an even interval between the dark and light parents.

The two descendant grays are placed next to each other in the center of the illustration. The difference between them is much more apparent than when each is seen as the center of a series.

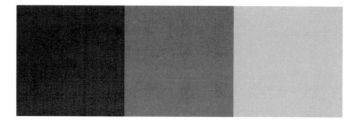

between. The important thing about even intervals is that the visual midpoint or middle mix be just that, no closer to one parent than to the other.[5]

Intervals aren't limited to the three steps of parent-descendant color mixtures. That three-part series can be part of, or a starting point for, a long progression of intervals. In a series of even intervals, each step is the visual midpoint of the sample on either side of it. Even intervals play such a major role in color study and color harmony that the word interval alone is sometimes used to mean a visually equidistant step.

Intervals can be deliberately uneven (closer to one parent than to the other). Tilting a middle color closer to one parent color than to the other is a technique used frequently by artists and illustrators to create special effects or illusions.[6]

Figure 2–3 *Intervals in Series.* In a series of even intervals, each step is the midpoint between the sample on either side of it.

Naming Colors

Each person's idea of the name of any color is just as individual as that person's ability to see differences between colors. In perceiving color, the retina of the eye receives the visible light and transmits the message or impulse to the brain. After the retina-to-brain message is transmitted, the brain forms an idea or name for the message.

Just as no one can know precisely what another person sees, no one can experience anyone else's idea of a specific color. If a teacher asks ten students to imagine a perfect red apple, and an apple appears magically above each head, the teacher will see ten red apples, each a slightly different red from the others.

Individuals are capable of seeing hundreds of possible reds and unconsciously expect that each is a fixed color with its own name. If a teacher presents to a class a single red apple, and asks the students to

. . . .

[5]For all of the reasons discussed later in this chapter, members within a group will rarely agree on the perfect visual midpoint between any two samples.

[6]Some of these illusions appear in Chapter 6, Using Color.

name the red, responses will be as prompt as they are varied—bright red, apple red, pure red, true red, and so on. And each student will passionately defend his or her name for that red as the correct one.

The Origins of Confusion: Color Names

Only a fraction of the words used to describe color are part of the history of languages. Most are modern and their origin is known. Some names derive from the pigments or dyes used to produce them. Ocher, umber, lamp black, zinc white, and lapis are examples. Other color names are completely unrelated to visual experience. They may be references to art of a particular culture, place, or time (Chinese Red, Venetian Red) or artist (Titian Red). Other colors are peculiarly named after historical events or public figures. "Magenta" was named in honor of a military victory; "Alice Blue" was a color favored by Teddy Roosevelt's daughter. Can anyone living today identify "Alice Blue"? An enormous group of color names relates to food. It's commonplace to buy a sweater or a car in lime, eggplant, lemon, banana, almond, mint, apricot, peach, or watermelon (but never in chicken, lamb chop, broccoli, or cabbage).

In the early 1930s The National Bureau of Standards tried to categorize and describe ten million colors for scientific and industrial use. The result was a massive color-name encyclopedia and a breathtaking failure. The group grayish-yellowish-pink, for example, included about thirty-five thousand samples (Sloane 1989).

Advertising copy is a major contemporary source of color names. The overt message is to communicate a color using words, but the concealed intent is the enhancement of a product image. The descriptive word or phrase may or may not be useful in helping to communicate color reality. The advertising vocabulary of color is a romantic one, not a practical one. It is creative writing.

There must be a universal frustration at being unable to name specific color samples. One researcher estimates that there are more than seven million different names for colors from industry or advertising copy. And the seven million names don't even approach the number of possible color variations. Computers can now produce 16 million variations in colors.

Even if every possible color appeared the same all the time and had a fixed name, could anyone memorize 7, 10, or 16 million names? Could anyone even think up 16 million names? Trying to name all possible color variations is about as productive as medieval debates to determine how many angels could dance on the head of a pin.

Even a dictionary is no help in establishing color names. There are no synonyms for color names in the dictionary. There are only references to the reader's own visual experience, like "yellow: the color of ripe lemons" (*The Random House Dictionary of the English Language* 1967).

What "yellow" really represents is a large group of colors containing more yellow than anything else, and individual ideas and memory; "yellow" associations.

Because every person both sees and thinks of colors slightly differently, no color name or word can ever have exactly the same meaning for everyone. But no one would call a red apple blue or green. In every language there's a universally accepted range of collective visual experience. The broadest categories of color are family names. A red apple is simply more red than it is anything else and is never called or mistaken for another hue. Yellow, red, blue, or any other color names are not fixed colors or specific variations or nuances of colors. *Red, orange, yellow, green, blue,* and *violet* (or purple) are words for enormous families of related colors.[7]

Restricting the names for colors to these six is important in color study because it helps students to focus on the visual experience. Professional designers use (and need to use) romantic and distinctive words for colors, despite their inherent instability of meaning, because the evocative and associative power of words plays a major role in marketing. Both ways of naming colors have equal weight in a designer's education as long as the critical difference between the two is recognized: the six hues of color study deal with eye-training, color recognition, and color use; the many color names of industry are about product image and sales.

Adaptation

Some aspects of color perception are determined by the structure of the eye and the nature of vision. Other aspects of color perception are more psychological in origin. For example, naming colors (carrying past visual experience and ideas to new visual experience) has a strong psychological component.

One aspect of color perception controlled by the physiology of the eye is adaptation. Adaptation is the eye's involuntary response to the quantity of available light. The rods and cones in the retina respond selectively to available light.

Rods control vision in dim light and perception is in shades of gray.

Cones take over in brighter light and color is seen. Color perception is actually dependent on cones.

Color perception lessens in dim light (objects appear grayer) because rods dominate vision, and increases (objects appear more color-

. . . .

[7]See Chapter 5, Color Description, for a discussion of pure colors.

ful) in higher lighting levels as cones dominate. Both rods and cones are always at work. It is almost as if there were two separate systems, one for day and one for night. As available light becomes less or more, the eye adapts quickly to the changing quantity by allowing one or the other to dominate vision.

The apparent change in colors caused by adaptation is not affected by the kind of light source present. The eye's response "cones for color, rods for gray tones" is the same for sunlight, candlelight, or fluorescent or incandescent light.

Memory Color

A wholly psychological influence on color perceptions is a kind of expectation called memory color. What is unconsciously assumed or remembered about an object—the "orange" of an orange or the "red" of an apple—will influence observation. A viewer influenced by memory color will report having seen and may even illustrate a preconceived idea about color. What is expected is reported by words or illustration even if the reality is different.

Color Constancy

Memory color affects observation of an object of familiar coloration. Color constancy is a second and equally powerful form of expectation. Color constancy means that the eye and brain adapt to all general light sources as if they were the same. Familiar objects and locations retain their identity under different conditions. The same colors seen in a room during the day and at night under incandescent light may be dramatically different, but the ordinary viewer is not conscious of those differences. Because colors have been experienced in one way, both individually and in relation to each other, the mind's image will override what is actually seen.

Another kind of visual accommodation occurs within groups of very close colors. Colors will often present as being similar or identical whether or not this is actually the case. In an all-white kitchen, the white of the refrigerator, the counters, the cabinets, and the ceiling paint may all be somewhat different, but the immediate cumulative effect will be that they are the same.

Constant, conscious color analysis would be exhausting on a daily basis. Adaptation, color memory, and color constancy make living with color a reflexive experience, not a conscious one. They simplify and edit what is seen. Because they are forgiving of poor color use, they play a large and proper role in the visual comfort level of living with color.

References

Goldstein, E. Bruce. 1984. *Sensation and Perception.* Belmont, California: Wadsworth Publishing Company.

The Random House Dictionary of the English Language. 1967. Editor in Chief Jess Stein. New York: Random House, Inc.

Sloane, Patricia. 1989. *The Visual Nature of Color.* New York: Design Press.

What is Color Study?

The ability to use color effectively, like drawing, is a skill that can be taught and strengthened. Color study begins with eye-training exercises. Sharpened color-discrimination skills make differences between colors more apparent and a particular vocabulary is needed to describe those differences. These beginning steps in color study, eye-training and a new vocabulary, are covered in Chapter 5, Color Description.

The second step in color study is to learn how and why colors will change when they are placed in different relationships to each other. Will a dark gray circle laid on black paper appear darker or lighter laid against yellow paper? Will a green sample seem bluer next to violet or next to orange? Understanding, predicting, and controlling how colors change because of placement is covered in Chapter 6, Using Color.

Mastering color description and color use isn't related to design ability. It's more like bicycle riding. Almost anyone can learn it. Once learned, it's never forgotten, although some people need more time and practice to get it right than others do. As long as there is color there will be new ideas about how to study it, but the basics of color description and control are well established and understandable.

The final area of study is also a goal, the creative use of color. Exploring creative color use, of course, is a lifetime occupation. The possibilities are limitless, but there are dependable guidelines for using color to achieve visual impact and color harmonies. Guidelines for using color creatively are discussed in Chapter 7, Color Harmony/Color Effect.

Color Theory: A Brief History

Most design programs require a foundation color course called Color I, Color Theory, Color Studio, or any of a dozen other names. These studio courses include exercises in color description, interaction and control, and color use. The hands-on studio approach is so natural to the subject that it's startling to learn that color study was once, and sometimes still is, the province not of artists but of scientists and philosophers.

One way to attempt to understand color is to try to systematize it—to hypothesize and illustrate a structured model of color sequences or relationships. The color-order model is a thread that runs from the earliest writings on color to the absolute present to tomorrow. Someone always has had, will have, and plans to have a new, positively definitive, absolutely true, undeniably logical, *right* way to organize color.

Old, new, or reconditioned, no color-order system is flawless or even comprehensive. Each tends to emphasize one aspect of color over the others. As a result, color systems fall fairly neatly into the following three groups:

>   technical systems

>   commercial sample systems

>   intellectual/philosophical systems

Technical Systems

Technical systems lie in the province of science and industry. They deal principally with light source colors. One means of measuring color is by determining the exact temperature of a piece of metal called a blackbody as it heats up. The color of a blackbody changes at specific points in degrees Kelvin (K). Color temperature refers to the point at which the blackbody is red, yellow, and so forth. In another instance of science-oriented color measurement, an organization called The International Commission on Illumination has developed a color triangle that locates mathematically the color (in degrees K) of any light source. Another system, the Color Rendering Index (CRI) compares how a given light source changes eight specified pastel colors against a standard indicator.

Technical systems measure under limited conditions. All operate within a very narrow range. Most deal with colors of light, not the colors of objects. Although the information provided is extremely accurate, little is useful to artists or designers, even in characterizing how "natural" or "unnatural" colors will appear. The technical systems of color organization aren't especially relevant to design professionals, although they can be of enormous use in ensuring quality control in manufacturing.

Commercial Sample Systems

There are dozens of currently available commercial color systems, like Pantone products or Color-aid® papers, that have been devised specifically for use by artists and designers. Color-aid® papers are silk-screened opaque colors printed on a high-quality paper suitable for art work or color exercises. The colors are very consistent between printings and papers are available in sets of various sizes or as individual sheets. PANTONE®* Colors are standards of the printing and graphic arts industries. Pantone, Inc. offers a broad range of high-quality products, from translucent color papers to markers, dyes, and printer's inks. Again, samples have a high degree of consistency. It's possible to call from New York to Osaka, ask for a design printed in a specified color, and get the expected result. (See Figure 3–1.)

Color sample systems are an aid in specifying colors or colorants. They don't claim to include all possible colors, but attempt to cover enough for most design needs, at least within one or two related industries. These sample systems are practical in intent and in fact. They don't contribute to an understanding of color, but they were never intended to do so. They offer a limited sampling of colors in a finite

. . . .

*Pantone, Inc.'s check-standard trademark for color reproduction.

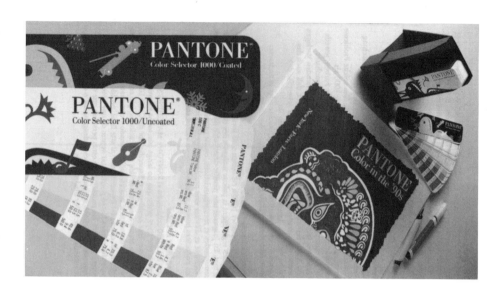

Figure 3–1 *Commercial Sample Systems.* PANTONE MATCHING SYSTEM offers designers an extensive range of colors available in a variety of art supplies and printers' inks.

number of color family groups. Within their limits they are useful tools and first class production aids.

Intellectual/Philosophical Systems

A fascination with color has never been limited to artists. Plato and Aristotle wrote on color—their works were known during the Renaissance. Artists have always written on color, but the great explosion of interest in color began in the intellectual ferment of the late seventeenth century.

The seventeenth and eighteenth centuries in Europe were a historical period known as the Enlightenment. During the Enlightenment there was a fresh and vigorous search for rational rather than mystical explanations for all kinds of phenomena. People began to believe in the existence of irrefutable laws of nature. This search for causes was as rigid and uncompromising in its way as the demands of absolute faith that preceded it. Only the source of authority had changed from God and his earthly representatives, the clergy, to reason and its earthly representatives, men.

The intellectual world of the eighteenth century was quite fluid. People didn't think of themselves as writers, biologists, or mathematicians but as "natural philosophers," theologians," or "geometricians" all with wide-ranging and overlapping areas of interest. Poets and literary figures wrote confidently, if with dubious expertise, on all kinds of scientific topics.

Most of those who first studied and wrote on color in this period were not artists. Poets poised at the edge of the sciences; they sought a rational basis for the nature of beauty itself and, as a corollary, color. In this way the "behavior" of colors could be explained and predicted and the mystery of observed color phenomena mastered by an understanding of natural laws.

Two themes dominated eighteenth- and nineteenth-century color study—the search for a perfect color-order system and the search for laws of harmony in color combinations. Just as there are classics in literature, there are classics of color writing. These treatises, written from the late eighteenth through the twentieth centuries, make up the collective body of knowledge called *Color Theory*.

In eighteenth century two towering and very different figures dominated the study of color—Isaac Newton (1642–1727) and Johann von Wolfgang Goethe (1749–1832). Newton, working at Cambridge in the late 1690s, first split sunlight into its component wavelengths by passing it through a prism. Newton observed that as each wavelength enters a prism it bends or refracts. Because glass, the material of the prism, slows each wavelength down at a slightly different rate, each emerges as a visibly separate beam of light, a different color. Newton recombined the separate beams with a lens and reconstituted white light. From this he hypothesized the nature of light and the origins of perceived color. He published his results, entitled *Opticks*, in 1703. Newton's conclusion that light alone generates color remains a basis of modern physics.

A rainbow is a naturally occurring demonstration of Newton's experiment. Tiny droplets of water in the atmosphere act as tiny prisms and sunlight is broken into colors. Newton reported seven distinct colors with his prism—red, orange, yellow, green, blue, indigo (blue-violet), and violet. Many people can't detect indigo as a separate color between blue and violet. A possible explanation for Newton's choice of a seven-hue spectrum of light is that he had unusual visual acuity in the blue-violet range. The more likely explanation is that despite his genius and the intellectual climate around him, Newton was a product of the seventeenth century. Mysticism was a great part of the climate of his time. A plausible theory is that he elected to have seven colors because of mystical properties associated with the number seven. Whatever the reason, the seven colors of the physical (light) spectrum persist in recognition of his discovery.

Newton's contemporaries viewed *Opticks* as a work on the nature of color, not on the nature of light. By the time of Newton's death in 1727, interest in *Opticks* was widespread. The ideas in it generated tremendous controversy all over Europe (Nicolson 1966). In 1731 J. C. LeBlon discovered and wrote a treatise on the primary nature of red, yellow, and blue in mixing pigments for painting. This was the first concept of three primary colors[1] and his work attracted a great deal of attention and acceptance (Birren 1987, 11). Unlike the theories of Newton, which concerned light, and the later ones of Goethe, which concerned percep-

. . . .

[1]Goethe later suggested that two primary colors, yellow and blue, were the basis for all others, but LeBlon's three primaries have prevailed as the convention for artists' colors.

tion and aesthetics, LeBlon's observations were about the practical reality of mixing paints.

Johann von Wolfgang Goethe was fascinated with color. He was familiar with Newton's theories of color, but was strongly opposed to them. "A great mathematician was possessed with an entirely false notion on the physical origin of color, yet, owing to his great authority as a geometer, the mistakes that he committed as an experimentalist long became sanctioned in the eyes of a world ever fettered in prejudices" (Goethe 1971, 163).

Goethe spent a great deal of energy trying to prove that Newton was wrong and published his first treatise (of a lifelong series intended to refute Newton and his hypotheses) entitled "Announcement for a Thesis in Color" in 1791 (Goethe 1971, 13). Goethe viewed colors not as light, but as an entity of their own, as experienced reality. His difficulties with Newton's ideas are evident in his own words. Newton's theory, he said, "does not help us to perceive more vividly the world around us" so that "Even if we found a basic phenomenon, even then, the problem remains that we would not want to accept it as such" (Lecture 1941, 4, 5). And, "Things which belong together according to our senses often lose their connections once we look into their causes" (Lecture 1941, 6). In addition, Goethe criticized Newton sharply for his views, "The natural philosopher should leave the elementary phenomena in their eternal quietness and pomp" (Lecture 1941, 5). Goethe was really saying, "Don't fool around with Mother Nature." His response to Newton was pragmatic. In effect he said, "What you say may or may not be true, but it certainly isn't useful in real life."

Like Newton, Goethe was both a genius and a child of the Enlightenment. Unlike Newton, he wrote with a sort of shotgun approach, aiming his considerable intellect at a topic, letting a lot of ideas fly, then turning without pause to fire again in a different direction. For twentieth-century readers, his writing includes a lot of unintended humor, like the discussion of the color sensibilities of earthworms and butterflies (Goethe 1971, 250).

Associations of color and beauty with morality were also a part of the Goethe's treatises. There were sinful colors and chaste ones. He associated moral character not only with choice of colors in clothing, but with skin color as well (Goethe 1971, 252–257).[2]

Despite the free-wheeling style and distractions, Goethe's observations were wide-ranging and seminal. What we call complementary colors, he called, with enormous insight, "completing colors" (Goethe 1971, 55).[3] He reported the phenomena of simultaneous contrast and

. . . .

[2]Sad to say, unconscious origins of racism can be found in the early writings of many nineteenth- and twentieth-century color theorists.

[3]See "Complementary Colors, Equilibrium, and Simultaneous Contrast" in Chapter 5.

afterimage extensively.[4] He recognized that no pure color exists except in theory and characterized the principal contrasts of color as polarity (contrast or opposition) and gradation (intervals).

Color writers after Goethe expand his ideas and contribute new material and ideas, but Goethe's observations were so wide-ranging, so fundamental, that almost every concept in modern color study can be found in his work. Goethe's most familiar and enduring contribution to color study is his circular six-hue spectrum of perceived color, which we know as the artists' spectrum—red, orange, yellow, green, blue, and violet.[5] The elegant simplicity of Goethe's spectrum can be described as perfect visual logic and from this six-hue spectrum he hypothesized rules of order, symmetry, and balance for harmonious combinations of colors.[6] (See Figure C–1.)

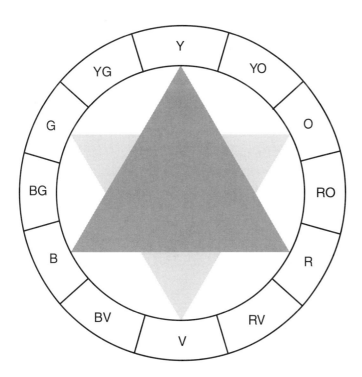

Figure 3–2 *The Artists' Spectrum.* Red, yellow, and blue are the primary colors; orange, green, and violet are the secondary colors.

. . . .

[4]See "The Artists' Spectrum" in Chapter 5.

[5]Newton had earlier recognized a visual (rather than a scientific) link between red and violet (or purple) and had devised the first color circle showing that relationship.

[6]Goethe believed that there were only two primary colors, blue and yellow (Goethe 1971, 55), and that all colors derived from them. Today we use Goethe's spectrum and LeBlon's concept of three primaries together.

Newton, Goethe, Science, Art, and Common Sense

Goethe's six-hue spectrum remains the convention for artists; Newton's seven-hue model of the full range of visible hues remains the scientist's physical spectrum. Probably because the students who pursue sciences are rarely the same ones who go into the visual arts, the differences between the two ideas of the full range of visible hues generally go unremarked.

We know that the earth is round, but our senses tell us that it's flat. We function on earth according to that sense of flatness, but we accommodate its roundness in our understanding. We accept in the same way the fact that color is only light, not a tangible reality. Nevertheless, we experience color in a direct and powerful way because it's very hard to deny the experience of our senses. We believe our eyes.

The battle over Newton's and Goethe's color theories was a major schism in the history of ideas. It wasn't necessary. Both theories are valid, but *each describes a different reality.*

Newton was looking at causes.

Goethe was looking at effects.

Artists and designers deal with effects, not causes. The interaction of light and color is a constant so it's critical that designers understand the effects of light. In understanding color we don't deny scientific reality, but in working with color we sometimes ignore it. Just as we act as if the world were flat, we work with color from the evidence of our senses.

Following Newton and Goethe

Although color order systems are a dominant theme in color study, Goethe's French contemporary Michel Eugene Chevreul (1786–1889) (!) addressed color in a different way. Chevreul was Master of the Gobelin Tapestry works. At some point he found difficulties with black dyes which seemed to lose their depth or darkness when placed next to other colors. Chevreul accepted the three-primary color theory. He observed and reported at length the phenomenon of simultaneous contrast. His 1839 *The Principles of Harmony and Contrast of Colors and Their Applications to the Arts (De La Loi du Contraste Simultane des Coleurs)* was a profound influence on painters of his time and a theoretical foundation of Impressionism.

Unlike the observer and chronicler Chevreul, most who followed returned to the scientific model and codified their observations into systems. The stress was on rules, control, and order. Artists and scientists still wrote as if on the same topic—color as order, as discipline, as scientific truth.

In *A Grammar of Colors* (1921), American Albert Munsell (1858–1918) devised an ingenious color tree with infinite room for expansion. Colors are organized by hue, value, and chroma (saturation). Each color is assigned a place on an alphanumeric (letter and number) scale. Munsell's system is still in use in many American and British schools today. The Munsell system is a rational one, but it gets lost in its labelling obsession. Munsell stated, "Naturally, every point (of color) has a defined number" (Munsell 1969, 10).[7] Munsell's theory is further weakened by his distracting associations of colors and morals; like Goethe he associated color choices with moral character.

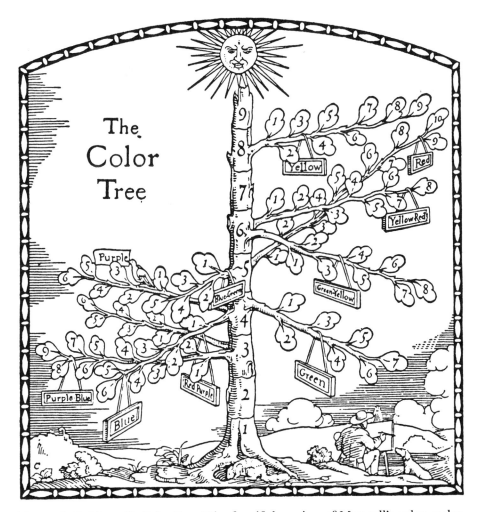

Figure 3–3 *Munsell's Color Tree.* The fanciful version of Munsell's color-order system shows how he imagined hue, value, and saturation in three dimensions.

. . . .

[7]Even if it were true, does it matter? Would a number or letter extend our understanding?

Almost simultaneously, German chemist Wilhelm Ostwald (1853–1932), a Nobel prizewinner, brought a conceptual color solid originally hypothesized by others to full-blown theory in *Color Science* (1923, translation 1931). Ostwald's later *The Color Primer* (1969), with an eight-hue spectrum, became mandatory in German and many English schools and was a powerful influence on the artists of the Bauhaus movement.

Wilhelm von Bezold (1837–1907) and Ludwig Von Helmholtz (1821–1894) contributed scientific fact to the growing body of color writing. The psychology and physiology of color vision became of increasing concern to scientists.

By the early twentieth century color had become an enormous and wide-ranging topic, positioned uncomfortably with one foot in the sciences and the other in the arts. It remained for the artists and designers of The Bauhaus, a design group founded in Weimar by German architect Walter Gropius in 1919, to end this ambiguity.

The Bauhaus group brought the study of color to a level of attention not seen since Goethe's challenge to Newton. Feininger, Klee, Kandinsky, Itten, Albers, and Schlemmer, master-students of color and color theory, addressed color from new directions with intelligence, wit, and energy. Although inevitably some elements of the old (quasi-scientific) style encroached in their writing, a definitive break was made between the study of color as science and the study of color as art and aesthetics. Light remained in the realm of physics; chemistry and engineering took over the nature of colorants; psychology, physiology, and medicine became the arena for perception.

Johannes Itten (1888–1967) echoed Goethe in defining color as a series of contrast systems and opposing forces.[8] Certainly he touched upon the eighteenth-century tradition as he codified color harmonies as a sort of geometry and suggested color chords and formulae for pleasing combinations of colors. But Itten based his conclusions on the observation of color phenomena. He established seven visual contrasts of color, separating both from the sciences and more rigid color-order systems. Significantly, Itten's major work is titled *The Art of Color* (1961).

It remained for Itten's colleague at The Bauhaus, Josef Albers (1888–1976), to make the final break with the color-order tradition. Albers fled Nazi Germany in the early 1930s and brought his teaching methods to Yale. He became the most influential name in color theory in the United States, but his book *Interaction of Color* (1963) contains no concepts of systems or structures. Albers did not need to contribute to ideas of color order. He had a new role to play. Josef Albers taught that true understanding of color comes from an intuitive approach to studio exercises. He stressed the instability and relativity of perceived colors and the power of visual training. At the same time, he taught that even within this unstable idea of color, predictable effects exist and can be

. . . .

[8]Itten's contrasts were hue, value (light/dark), saturation (dull/vivid), warmth/coolness, complementary contrast, simultaneous contrast, and contrast of extension (area).

controlled.[9] In *Interaction of Color* (1963), Albers casually discounts the benefits of the generations of theory that preceded him, "This book . . . reverses this order and places practice before theory, which is, after all, the conclusion of practice" (Albers 1963, 1). For Albers, the visual experience was paramount.

Color Study Today

There is now and ever will be an endless and growing diversity in approaches to teaching color from wholly intuitive systems to rigidly mathematical ones. Each is only a theory developed to support someone's pet hypothesis. *There are no unbiased systems in color organization.* Albers' *Interaction of Color* (1963) was revolutionary and gained wide acceptance in the United States, but there was no total rout of earlier teaching methods. Some schools continue to teach color courses based on Munsell's system; others use a combined curriculum.

Josef Albers was familiar with the writings of Newton, Goethe, Chevreul, Ostwald, Itten, Kandinsky, and others. He diverged from the long and well-trod path of the color theorists in a more fundamental way than many of his contemporaries, but his new direction grew from a strong foundation in the past. The Albers intuitive approach, used alone, dominates American color education today. Detached from its background and separated from history, it is less accessible to students than it can be. The intuitive approach makes infinitely more sense when it follows an understanding of what color-order systems are about. By learning first to discriminate hue, value, and saturation and mastering the idea of intervals, students acquire skills that make the Albers exercises comprehensible from the start. Color order and the Albers intuitive approach are not alternative ways to study color, nor are they competitive. The first leads seamlessly to the second and together they embrace an understanding of color without limits or gaps.

This book uses the (Goethe) artists' spectrum of six hues (red, orange, yellow, green, blue, and violet) as its color-organization convention because it is familiar, simple, and universally recognized. Whenever the word spectrum (or the phrase color wheel or color circle) is used below it refers to the artists' spectrum. (See Figure C–1.)

The colors and sequences of colors described and discussed are subtractive mixtures and perceived colors—effects, not recipes for mixing paints or other colorants. When we see color

Light is the cause.

Colorants are the means.

The color we see is the effect.

. . . .

[9]No attempt is made here to list all major writers on color.

Class Action: Studying Color in a Group

Because color perception is influenced by forces of physiology and psychology and no two individuals see or share the exact idea of any given color, it's easy to conclude that color study in a class would be at best a waste of time or at worst a scheduled free-for-all. But there are great benefits from studying color in a group. For every problem assigned there are wrong answers, but there are also many different possible right answers. Twenty students may bring in twenty different, equally acceptable, solutions to the same color assignment.

Academic (non-design) education tends to reward students who find the single "right" answer to a question or assignment. The possibility of many right answers for each problem is extraordinarily liberating because it increases exponentially the chances of success. It is also extraordinarily instructive because seeing a variety of responses, even "wrong" ones, sharpens developing critical skills.[10]

When there is an irreconcilable difference of opinion in class, it's usually about the nature of a very small difference between close colors. Differences in visual acuity and ideas of color will always have this result so students sometimes must learn to "agree to disagree" for a particular problem. Disagreement about names of color samples is eliminated by reducing the names for hue to only six—red, orange, yellow, green, blue, and violet.

Because color study starts with the narrowest range of ideas and expands to encompass all possibilities, students with a self-assessed "strong sense of color" or creative bent may be inhibited, disoriented, or just plain exasperated at the start. Just as mastering written music will initially slow down a natural musician, learning the language of color may temporarily hamper the artist or designer. The inhibiting effect is short term. There is a moment when learned material becomes reflexive like the magical moment for children when learning to read ends and reading begins. Understanding color begins and ends with one conscious effort—to see colors without the interference of preconceived ideas.

References

Albers, Josef. 1963. *Interaction of Color.* New Haven, Connecticut: Yale University Press.

Birren, Faber. 1987. *Principles of Color.* West Chester, Pennsylvania: Schiffer Publishing Company.

. . . .

[10]Some students who have been very successful in traditional academic areas find this flexible standard of "rightness" very difficult at first.

The Color Theories of Goethe and Newton in the Light of Modern Physics. Lecture held in Budapest on April 28, 1941 at the Hungarian Club of Spiritual Cooperation. Published in German in May, 1941 in the periodical "Geist der Zeit." English translation courtesy of Dr. Ivan Bodis-Wollner, Rockefeller University, New York, 1985.

Goethe, Johann von Wolfgang. 1971. *Goethe's Color Theory.* Translated by Rupprecht Matthei. New York: Van Nostrand Reinhold.

Itten, Johannes. 1961. *The Art of Color.* Translated by Ernst Van Haagen. New York: Van Nostrand Reinhold.

Itten, Johannes. 1970. *The Elements of Color.* Edited by Faber Birren. Translated by Ernst Van Haagen. New York: Van Nostrand Reinhold.

Munsell, Albert Henry. 1969. *A Grammar of Colors.* New York: Van Nostrand Reinhold.

Ostwald, Wilhelm. 1969. *The Color Primer.* New York: Van Nostrand Reinhold.

Chapter 4

Tools of the Trade

Media / Recipes: Mixing Colors / Tinting Strength / Dyes,
Pigments, and Process Colors / Color Papers / Selecting Media

Media

We know that light is the cause of color and that what we see is the effect. A medium is the means from light to effect—the specific substance that reacts to light and gives us color. A *medium* is a liquid, paste, wax, or other base into which colorants are introduced. The base is a vehicle for transferring colorants. Together, base and colorant are a medium. Each medium has its own range of colors. There may be an enormous range of available colors, like oil paints, or a limited range of very similar colors, like Conte crayons.

Design professionals use all sorts of media to produce their work. Every medium has a surface quality of its own—rough, opaque, reflective, sparkling, clear, gritty. A medium is selected both for its visual qualities and because it is appropriate to the material it will color. Except as an experiment, no one would use watercolor on blackboard or oil paint on tissue paper.

There's an enormous and ever-growing list of media. Many designs are produced using mixed media, like pen and ink with water color or colored pencil and marker. Media range from poster paints, water color, gouache, casein, oils, acrylics, marker, charcoal, crayons, graphite pencil, colored pencil, pastel, oil pastel, and ink to dyes and printing inks.

Fluorescent or "Dayglo" colors in a variety of media are more than highly reflective. They contain special colorants that absorb wavelengths of light from above the range of the visible spectrum and reemit it at a lower range as visible light. This added light emission makes them highly visible against any background.

Recipes: Mixing Colors

Within a single medium there may be a number of tubes or jars with different names (for example, Periwinkle Blue, Ultramarine, Cerulean Blue, Indigo, Myosotis Blue, Prussian Blue) which produce similar or seemingly identical colors. One brand of gouache (opaque water color) has five "reds" with different tube names, all of which appear identical when used directly from the tube. In spite of the apparent similarity, each reacts differently when combined with other colors in the same medium.

Two or more colorants work together to produce a new color in a simple way. Most colorants reflect light in at least two wavelengths of light and may reflect more than two. One wavelength will be reflected most strongly so that the secondary wavelengths present are not really visible to the naked eye. It's rare to find a colorant that reflects only one wavelength or color.

A red colorant may absorb blue, green, violet, and yellow wavelengths and some of the orange; it will reflect red and a little orange.

The orange may not be visible to the naked eye. A yellow colorant may absorb blue, red, green, violet, and some of the orange; it will reflect yellow and some of the orange. Again, that orange may not be visible to the naked eye. When the red and yellow are mixed, each will continue to absorb the same colors they absorbed when used alone. The only color that will be reflected is orange—the one that both paints reflect in common. If the paints do not have a common reflecting element they will always yield a muddy neutral when mixed no matter how brilliant they appear when used alone.

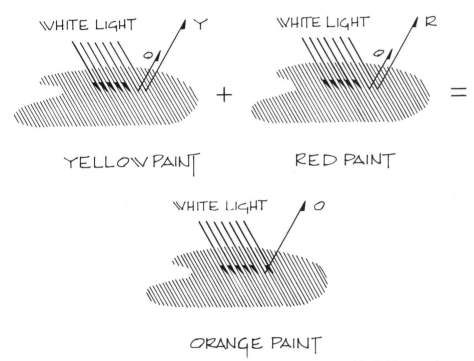

Figure 4–1 *Mixing Colorants.* Two paints mixed together will yield a new hue only when that hue is already present in each. If there is no common hue, mixing two paints will produce a tertiary (muddy or brown) result.

An experienced colorist makes a selection based not on the appearance of an unmixed color straight from the tube or jar, but on the mixing affinities of specific colors. Mixing affinities are like recipes. Two or more ingredients are mixed together for a predictable result. Color mixing can be learned by trial and error which is time-consuming and costly but interesting. Alternatively there are well-written books on color mixing, usually for specific media. And, of course, the mechanics of color mixing can be learned from a teacher or peer experienced in the medium.

Tinting Strength

Different hues within the same medium will also vary in *tinting strength*. Tinting strength means the relative quantity of the colorant needed to produce a perceptible difference when mixed into another color. In most media, for example, yellow has very little tinting strength. A mixture of one-half cup of yellow paint to one-half cup of green paint will result in little or no change to the green. But a teaspoon of green added to a cup of yellow usually produces an immediate change to yellow-green. In mixing colorants, quantity is no predictor of result; only tinting strength effects change.

Colorants with great tinting strength are like garlic. A teaspoon of garlic in an apple pie will certainly be noticed. On the other hand, a teaspoon of apple in a garlic puree won't make much of an impression.

Dyes, Pigments, and Process Colors

Dyes are colorants in solution; they are fully dissolved in water, alcohol, or other solvent. Some dyes are opaque and block all light from reaching the underlying material. Other dyes are translucent, the underlying material reflects the light back through them. When light is reflected back through a dye, as in a translucent ink on a white paper ground, the color effect is very light reflective and brilliant. Dyes penetrate the material they color and bond with it on the molecular level.

Pigments are finely ground particles of colorant suspended in a medium. They are typically more opaque and less brilliant than dyes. Pigments "sit" on a surface rather than bonding with it.

Traditionally, dyes were organic—derived from plant and animal material. Many were "fugitive," oxidizing (fading or altering in color) rapidly on exposure to light or air. Pigments were inorganic, ground from earth or semiprecious stones, and were more durable. Present-day chemistry and dyeing and printing techniques have made the old definitions of dyes and pigments obsolete. Just as textiles and construction materials now exist which are entirely man-made, man-made colorants now exist with brilliance and durability unimaginable years ago.

In the printing and reprographic industries, there are industry-specific colorants called process colors—cyan (blue-green), magenta (red-violet), and yellow. Process colors are special types of colorant available in a number of media such as drawing ink, printing ink, and marker.[1] (See Figure C–3).

In recipe terms, process colors are close to the perfect medium. They can be mixed to result in almost all possible colors, but all mixed

. . . .

[1] In this context these colors are sometimes referred to as "process primaries," "subtractive primaries," or "subtractive colors." Process magenta is sometimes called "process red" and cyan also called "process blue."

together they reach a neutral gray, not black. Four-color printing is done with the three process colors and the addition of black to give sharpness and depth to the image. Process colors are referred to as CMYK—cyan, magenta, yellow, and black (K).

Process colors available in artists' media are especially valuable in the preparation of artwork for printing because the design phase, although executed in a different medium, will closely approximate the finished printed material. (See Figure C–3.)

Color Papers

Silk-screen printed color papers, available in boxed sets of several hundred colors, are indispensable to beginning eye-training. Color paper has a disciplined simplicity. It offers a flat, opaque, matte surface. Painted samples may have texture and variation, but no texture disturbs the surface of printed color paper. Working from the paper samples allows repeated comparisons from fixed examples so a single color may reliably be observed in different placements. Color paper is also a good teaching tool because it forces choice. The number of colors in a paper set is limited so perfect answers (whatever they may be!) to assigned problems are often not possible. Forced choice compels closer analysis and closer analysis leads to greater understanding.

Painting color samples is vital to later exercises, but color papers offer a simpler and more secure starting point for beginning color study. If an assignment reads "illustrate the color between red and yellow," and the medium is poster paint, the result will be mud color instead of orange. (See "Recipes: Mixing Colors" on page 000.) Using colored paper eliminates the temptation to accept as satisfactory a visually poor result achieved by poor paint mixing.

Selecting Media

An orange and a violet mixed, dulled with gray and tinted with white, yield an exotic and nameless color. Like all colors it is a visual mix of red, yellow, blue, white, and black. In an imaginary world where everyone sees and thinks of each color in exactly the same way, there would be a perfect medium for illustrating colors. In this imaginary perfect medium, there would be only five pots of paint—red, yellow, blue, black, and white. In a perfect book on color, the illustrations would use this perfect medium. Students would do their color exercises in the perfect medium; then use it later in their various professions.

In the real world there's no universal or perfect medium. Ceramic glaze, watercolor, oil paint, acrylics, chalk, printers' ink, markers, and textile dye; each has its own set of visual qualities and technical boundaries. Selecting a medium means selecting a set of limitations.

Product design usually means design in one medium for final fabrication in another. Because there can be no perfect color rendition in one medium of the visual quality of another, the designer's rendering medium must be as carefully chosen as the colors. There's no point in presenting to a client a rendering of brilliant red dinnerware if no ceramic glaze can be found to produce the illustrated product.

The professional artist-designer identifies a visual goal—a color to be achieved—and mixes paints, dyes, glazes, or other colorants to reach that goal. Learning to mix paints or other colorants is not the same as learning to see differences, similarities, or intervals between colors. Color discrimination skills—the ability to identify the elements of visual mixes—are skills required in all design disciplines. The ability to create those hues in a given medium is a skill of each design profession.

Chapter **5**

Color Description

Everyone in the design industries must at times communicate color ideas in words. It's apparent that color names are poor verbal tools, but there is a practical vocabulary of color for design professionals. The effective way to describe colors and the differences between them is to describe differences in color qualities. Every color sample has three separate, distinct descriptive qualities:

Hue: the name of the dominant color of a sample—red, orange, yellow, green, blue, or violet

Value: relative lightness or darkness of a sample

Saturation: the hue-intensity or brilliance of a sample, its dullness or vividness

The words used to describe hue, value, and saturation are adjectives. They describe a quality that's present in a tangible something—a car, a dress, a cow, or just a paint sample on paper. The tangible something is implied when we say "yellow" or "blue" or "red." There is red light and red paint and red onion pie, but there is no object "red." The same is true for "dark" or (in the descriptive sense) "light," and for "dull" or "vivid." Each word describes something, whether that thing is stated or just implied. The qualities of hue, values, and saturation coexist in every color we see. They expand the description of any object. "This is my dark red shirt" gives two more ideas about my shirt than "this is my shirt."

The most important way in which concepts of hue, value, and saturation are used is to characterize differences between colors. Hue, value, and saturation are most effectively used as relative terms in comparing colors. Colors may be very similar or very different, but all possible differences between them can always be described using ideas of hue, value, or saturation. For example, "My new car is a light (value) gray-blue (saturation-hue), but I wish I had bought the dark (value) blue-green (hue) one instead."

Hue

Hue means the name of the color we see. There may be an endless number of hypothetically-possible individually-distinguishable hues, but every one of them can be described using one or two of only six words. The only words ever needed to describe the hue of any object are

Red   Orange   Yellow   Green   Blue   Violet

The word color is used interchangeably to mean hue.[1] *Chroma* is

....

[1]The word color is used conversationally to describe a complete sample, including its qualities of hue, value, and saturation. The answer to "what color is it?" can be pale gray-blue, which includes more ideas than just hue. It's also used to mean hue alone, but "color" is never used to describe value or saturation alone.

another synonym for hue and is part of some familiar color words:

chromatic	having hue
achromatic	having no discernible hue
polychromatic	having many hues
monochromatic	having one hue (but not necessarily only one value or level of saturation

A color is called by the name of its most obvious or dominant hue. We think of it as "being" that hue, but the names for colors are adjectives. Nothing "is" an adjective. Colors are hardly ever one single, definitive hue. They usually exist "between" color names. Is a red sample really red or is it red-orange or red-violet? Most disagreements arise over which word *best* describes a color.

Using the word "contains" is a nearly foolproof way to evaluate the hue content of any sample. Color samples "contain" hue qualities, usually more than one, so "this red contains some orange" is perfectly descriptive. Every color has a hue family, but no color has a fixed name. "Contains" is the most useful when one hue is compared to another. "This red contains more violet than that red" or "This green contains more yellow than the other one."

The Artists' Spectrum

The *artists' spectrum* is a circle that illustrates the full range of visible hues. Synonyms for the artists' spectrum are the *color wheel* or color circle. (See Figure C–1.) There are too many possible hues in the range of human vision to illustrate all of them easily in one circle so the spectrum is a sort of visual outline or synopsis. The simplest artists' spectrum includes the six named colors in even intervals of hue—red, orange, yellow, green, blue, and violet. The spectrum is often expanded from 6 to 12 steps, but no new color names are introduced to do so. The expanded artists' spectrum includes

Red	**Green**
Red-Orange	Blue-Green
Orange	**Blue**
Yellow-Orange	Blue-Violet
Yellow	**Violet**
Yellow-Green	Red-Violet

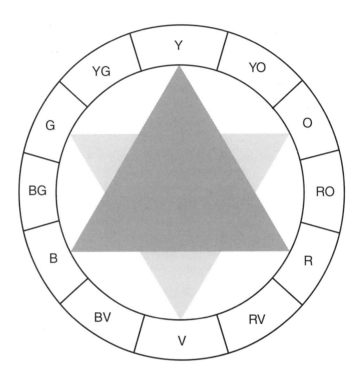

Figure 5–1 *The Artists' Spectrum.*

The color wheel is limited to 6 or 12 hues only because this is a concise, easily illustrated figure. The spectrum can be expanded to any number of hue intervals as long as the additional hues are inserted evenly in all hue ranges. There can be 6, 12, 24, 48, 96, or more hues, but not 37 or 51. The only limits to the number of places on a color wheel are the visual acuity of the viewer and the practical problems of illustrating it.

The artists' spectrum is circular and continuous; violet forms the bridge between red and blue. The spectrum of visible light (additive color) is linear, moving from short wavelengths of light (violet) to long ones (red).

Primary and Secondary Colors

Red, yellow, and blue are the *primary colors* of the artists' spectrum. They are the simplest hues. They cannot be broken down visually into other colors or reduced into component parts. They are the most different from each other because they have no elements in common. All other hues are derived visually from red, yellow, and blue.

Green, orange, and violet are the *secondary colors*. Each is the visual midpoint between two primary colors—an even interval between two primary parents. A secondary hue is visually 50 percent of the primary on either side of it.

Green is the middle mix of blue and yellow.

Orange is the middle mix of red and yellow.

Violet is the middle mix of blue and red.

Secondary colors are less contrasting in hue from one another than primary colors are because each pair of secondaries has a common primary.

Orange and violet both contain red.

Orange and green both contain yellow.

Green and violet both contain blue.

The third group of colors most commonly illustrated in a spectrum are the ones between a primary and a secondary. These are sometimes *incorrectly* called tertiary colors. Hues that lie between primary and secondary colors have no special category or name. They are sometimes described as *intermediate colors*.

Red-orange

Yellow-orange

Yellow-green

Blue-green

Blue violet

Red-violet

Like the secondary colors, they are the midpoints of colors on either side of them. Yellow-green, for example, is the even interval between the primary yellow and the secondary green.

The spectrum is fixed in its rotation or order of colors. Spectrums can be illustrated in a number of ways and still be correct. The medium chosen affects the final result a great deal. If the medium is water color, the colors will be relatively light and clear. A more opaque medium like gouache will establish a different set of intervals. As long as the hues are clearly identifiable, in the right sequence and the intervals well-spaced, color wheels can vary a great deal from each other and be equally true.

Saturated Color

A *saturated color* is a hue in its strongest possible manifestation. The reddest red or the bluest blue imaginable are saturated colors. Saturated colors are also called *pure colors* or *full colors*. Saturated colors are said to be at maximum chroma. Saturated colors aren't limited to the 6 or 12 hues of the artists' spectrum. *Any hue inserted at any point between saturated hues on the color wheel is also a saturated hue.* A saturated hue can contain one or two primaries in any mix or proportion, but never includes the third primary. Saturated or pure colors are additionally defined by a negative—by what they do not contain. Saturated colors are hues undiluted by black, white, or gray.

Imagine the full range of saturated colors as the color wheel with each color blending into the next like a rainbow. Any point on that circle is a saturated color. Red-red-orange or blue-blue-green are saturated colors as certainly as are red, orange, blue, or green. As long as a color contains only one or two primaries and is undiluted by black, white, or gray, it is a saturated color. The only limit to the number of saturated colors is the limit of human color vision.

Other Spectrums, Other Primaries

The artists' spectrum illustrates one color-order system. It's familiar, visually logical, easy to represent as a two-dimensional figure, and allows for theoretically unlimited expansion. Many scientific and nonscientific disciplines use other spectrums to illustrate alternative color-order systems. Choosing one spectrum instead of another is exactly that—a choice. No spectrum is inherently more correct than another. The systems may vary in the names of colors, the number of colors illustrated (from three or four to infinite), and in the assignment of what might be called prime points on the wheel. Ostwald, for example, predicated an eight-hue spectrum that contained sea-green (blue-green) and leaf-green (yellow-green) (Ostwald 1969). Psychologists construct a four-hue spectrum with red, green, yellow, and blue as primaries.

These different color circles may appear at first to conflict, but they are all variants of the same color-order idea. All recognize the same sequence of colors—red, orange, yellow, green, blue, and violet. Hue intervals may be added or subtracted, but no spectrum moves from red to green or from orange to blue. Arguments made for the names or locations of primaries and secondaries are exercises in philosophy. In the end, all color wheels include the same colors and follow the same color-order rotation.

An argument is sometimes made for expanding the spectrum with more steps or intervals in the yellow-to-blue and yellow-to-red ranges than in the blue-to-red ones. A color wheel illustrated in this way has many more intervals in the yellow, oranges, and greens than in the reds, violets, or blues.

In infancy, before we can see hue, we are able to detect difference between dark and light. Our first experience of vision persists through life; the ability to see light/dark contrast almost defines vision. In color study, the contrast between light and dark is called *value*. Light colors are high in value; dark colors are low in value.

It's certainly true that a great many steps can be seen between yellow-to-red and yellow-to-blue. There is a great value difference between yellow and the other two primaries. Yellow is much lighter than blue or red so a range of intervals is easily perceived between them. Blue and red are closer in value so it's harder to detect intervals between them.

The purpose of the spectrum is to illustrate the full range of visible hues. No matter how many intervals are added in the spaces between yellow-and-red or yellow-and-blue, *no new hue is introduced*. Only intervals of value are added. To say that there are more steps of pure color between yellow-red and yellow-blue misunderstands the nature and purpose of the spectrum.[2]

Chromatic Scales

A linear series of hues that doesn't form a circle or wheel is a chromatic scale. A chromatic scale can be one of pure (saturated) colors or of more complex, diluted colors. Its defining characteristic is that each step in its progression is a change in hue. A hue series between blue and orange, for example, (blue/green/yellow/orange) is a chromatic scale but not a spectrum.

Warm and Cool Hues

Hues are sometimes described as warm or cool. Warm colors are reds, oranges, yellows, and intervals between them. Cool colors contain blue—blues, greens, violets, and the steps between them. Warm and cool are adjectives used to describe two characteristics of hue and the warmth or coolness of a hue is sometimes called its color temperature.[3]

The color wheel is weighted toward the warm colors. Only blue is cool while red and yellow are both considered warm. As a result the entire spectrum is more heavily "warm" than it is "cool." Of the six basic hues, blue is considered to be the polar extreme of cool and orange the polar extreme of warm.

Warmth and coolness in colors are not fixed qualities. The same sample can be warmer or cooler depending on its placement. Even primary colors are subject to variation in warmth or coolness. Reds can be cooler and warmer (closer to violet or closer to orange). It's possible

. . . .

[2]A spectrum illustrated in this way has an immediate problem in establishing complementary pairs. There are so many colors in the yellow ranges that they might actually end up opposite each other.

[3]Not to be confused with the scientific concept of color temperature, which refers to the temperature in degrees Kelvin (K) of a blackbody as it heats up and changes color.

to describe a sample of blue, a cool color, as warmer than another blue because it contains a bit of green and therefore a bit of yellow, which is warm.[4]

The terms cool and warm are helpful in describing families of colors and in comparison of samples for warmth and coolness alone. They are less useful terms when hue adjustment is important. Directing a color change toward a specific hue communicates more clearly. "This blue is too warm. Cool it off, get rid of the green. This yellow seems a little green. Warm it up, bring it closer to orange."

Analogous Colors

Analogous colors are colors next to each other on the spectrum. They are sometimes defined as a primary color, a secondary next to it, and hues between the two, but it's not necessary that a primary or secondary color be present for colors to be analogous. Blue-violet and blue-blue-violet are neither primaries nor secondaries, but they are next to each other on the spectrum and analogous.

Analogous colors are limited in range on the spectrum. One hue is present and dominant in all colors in the group. Analogous colors always contain two primary colors but never the third. Some examples are

Blue and green (50 percent or more blue in each)

Blue, blue-green, and green (50 percent or more blue in all)

Yellow and yellow-green (50 percent or more yellow in each)

Orange and yellow-orange (50 percent or more yellow in both)

Red, red-violet, and violet (50 percent or more red in each)

Defining analogy as colors between a primary and secondary restricts analogous colors to groups in which a primary dominates. In a more generous definition, some experts simply define analogy as colors adjacent on the color wheel and containing two, but never three, primaries. The alternative definition includes as analogous other close colors like those on either side of the secondaries,

Yellow-orange, orange, and red-orange (50 percent or more orange in each)

Red-violet, violet, and blue-violet (50 percent or more violet in each)

. . . .

[4]Blues can also move to red, the other warm pole, and have a violet overtone. There's no consensus on calling blues warm as they become more green or violet because some people consider violet-blues warm; others consider green-blues warm.

Analogy isn't confined to the pure colors. Saturated hues and muted ones, hues diluted by white or black, can also be analogous. No matter what the value or saturation of colors, only the relationship of hues between samples determines whether or not they are analogous. (See Figure C–6.)

Analogous color groupings are among the most frequently used in the design industries. An expanded view of analogy offers designers a richer palette of analogous colors, if not necessarily a traditionally defined one.

Complementary Colors

Complementary colors are any two hues opposite one another on the color wheel. Whether a spectrum is illustrated with 6 or 96 hues, a straight line drawn across the center of the circle will always connect complementary colors. Together the two are called complements or a complementary pair. The basic complementary pairs are

Red and green

Yellow and violet

Blue and orange

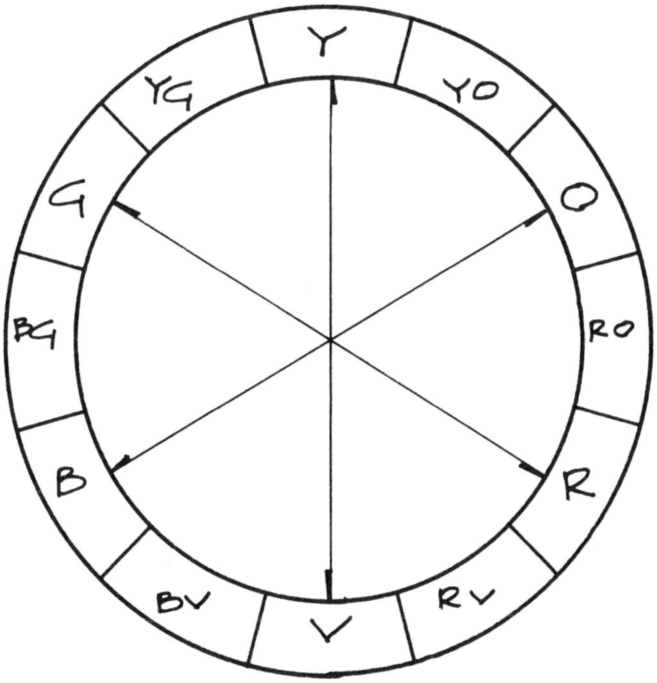

Figure 5–2 *Complementary Pairs.* Complements are opposites at any point on the spectrum. Only three pairs are indicated here.

Each pair of complementary colors contains all three primary colors. In the basic complementary pairs, one is a primary and the other two are mixed as a secondary.

Another way to define complements is to say that complements are a pair of colors that, when mixed, result in a complete lack of hue. This is true for visual mixes (the colors we imagine) and also for mixing complementary colors in paints. Mixed complements contain all three primaries so they will absorb all wavelengths of light.[5] (See Figure C–11.)

For every possible saturated color there is an opposite, its complement. All complements have the same attributes:

Used together as pure hues they are jarring and fatiguing to the eye.[6] (See Figure C–14.)

If complementary colors are mixed to the visual midpoint between them, the result is a complete loss of discernible hue, an achromatic mixture. Mixing complements is a way to mix three primary colors.[7]

Complementary contrast is the foundation of simultaneous contrast and afterimage.

The three basic complementary pairs are most different from each other in exactly the same way as the primaries. Neither half contains a hue in common with its opposite. All other complementary pairs are less contrasting because, like secondary colors, each half contains a common hue. Examples are

> Blue-green and red-orange
>
> > (each half contains some yellow)
>
> Yellow-green and red-violet
>
> > (each half contains some blue)
>
> Blue-violet and yellow-orange
>
> > (each half contains some red)

· · · · · · · · · · · · · · · · · · · ·

[5]This "mixing" definition of complements should never be used alone because in some media mixing noncomplements will do the same thing. Red and blue kindergarten poster paints mixed will produce an achromatic tone, but they are not complements. See "Recipes: Mixing Colors" on page 44.

[6]See "Equilibrium" on page 59.

[7]Combining complements to mute and darken hues is the classic mixing technique in almost all media.

Like analogous colors, samples don't have to be pure hues to be complementary. Complementary hues retain that relationship whether they are pure hues or have been diluted by black, white, or gray. The complementary relationship is critically important to vision, special effects and illusions, and color harmony.

Equilibrium

The theory of *equilibrium* states that when three primaries are present in the field of vision, the eye will be in a state of equilibrium or rest. Equilibrium isn't just a descriptive term. It's a physiological condition that the eye requires at all times.[8] When one or two of the primaries is missing in the field of vision, the eye will generate for itself the missing color or colors. It's not necessary for the primaries to be present in equal proportion for the eye to be at rest, just that all three be present in any mix or quantity.

There are endless possible primary combinations that the eye will accept to reach equilibrium—three primaries, two secondaries, complements, colors diluted by the complement or mixed as muted hues, and so on.[9] Any grouping or color which contains the three primaries in some way allows the eye to be at rest.

It may be technically true that the eye is at rest when ALL primaries are present in any form, but brilliant or saturated colors have an adverse affect on the sensory experience of equilibrium. A saturated color floods the eye with a great deal of a single or narrow range of wavelength(s). Three primaries in highly saturated or brilliant form can deliver separate, strong stimuli. The eye reacts to each as if it were an individual stimulus.[10] The involuntary effort to respond to contradictory stimuli, to maintain equilibrium, causes optical vibration, headache, blurred vision, or dizziness. No one would consider this "at rest." The state of rest is reached most fully when the three primaries are mixed in the literal sense—as paints or other media—into one or more muted hues. The slightest dulling of any pure color makes it less stimulating to the eye. The "earth" colors, muted almost to the point of achromaticity, may be so often used because they are genuinely physically restful.

. . . .

[8]Equilibrium actually depends on the presence of the additive primaries (colors of light) in the field of vision (red, green, and blue wavelengths). As a practical matter the subtractive primaries of red, yellow, and blue reflect the necessary wavelengths and are identical in effect.

[9]See "Tertiary Colors: Muted Hues and Brown" on page 63 and "Saturation" on page 71.

[10]The same is true for strong tints, hues diluted with a small amount of white.

Simultaneous Contrast

Simultaneous contrast occurs when the eye is not at rest. It's an involuntary response to hue stimulation. Because it is part of the eye's response to light, it can't be thought away or trained out, but an experienced colorist will be able to predict when it will occur and to select colors that will reduce or emphasize its impact.

Equilibrium is destroyed when one or two of the three primaries is missing in the field of vision. In the presence of a single hue, the eye will actually create the missing color or colors, the complement.

> For any given color, the eye generates the complement simultaneously and spontaneously.

The "missing" complement appears in any adjacent achromatic area. For example, a gray paper square laid on a red background will appear to take on a greenish quality. The same gray square laid on green will appear as a rosier gray. (See Figure C–16.)

The strongest effects of simultaneous contrast occur when the achromatic (influenced) color is laid directly on top of the stimulating (influencing) hue because the achromatic is completely surrounded. However, areas of adjacent color can influence each other very strongly. A true story illustrates how damaging unexpected simultaneous contrast can be.

> An interior designer selected a gray carpet for installation throughout an apartment. The client had been specific, "I hate blue, I only want gray." Together, the client and designer selected a gray carpet.

> The apartment walls were painted in variants of "peach" and "terra cotta" (tints and shades of orange). When the carpet was installed, it was a muted, but definite, blue.

> The frantic client brought a sample of the carpet back to the carpet showroom, insisting she had received the wrong goods. It was identical to her original selection.

Simultaneous contrast was the villain. The orange-based wall colors caused the eye to generate the complementary blue and the gray carpet was a perfect neutral area to receive that effect.

Simultaneous contrast is so pervasive that it's a factor in the selection of every neutral (including, and especially, whites) that will be placed near a single hue or family of hues.[11] Happily, unwanted effects

. . . .

[11] Acknowledging the indignation that consumers have voiced when they have painted walls "white" only to see them as "pink" when green carpet is installed, paint manufacturers now provide charts showing which whites should be used with green schemes, blue schemes, orange schemes, and so on. The colors are formulated to prevent the surprises caused by simultaneous contrast.

are easy to avoid. If a green textile is to be used against a white one, the white one must contain a trace of green to counteract the red that the eye will supply. Without the green undertone, the white will take on a pink cast. A red fabric calls for a warm undertone to negate the green that the eye will supply. If the designer in the previous example had used a warm gray carpet with an orange undertone, there would not have been a problem.

Although the effect of simultaneous contrast is strongest when the single hue is a saturated color or brilliant tint, colors don't have to be saturated for simultaneous contrast to occur. Muted, pale, or dark hues will also generate simultaneous contrast in a nearby achromatic area. Simultaneous contrast will occur when any single hue is adjacent to or on top of an achromatic area.

Afterimage and Contrast Reversal

Afterimage is the same phenomenon as simultaneous contrast but takes place under a more limited set of conditions. Simultaneous contrast occurs whenever there is a single stimulating hue and an adjacent achromatic area within the field of vision. In afterimage, the missing complement appears as a ghost image on an achromatic surface after the stimulating hue is taken away. For afterimage to occur, there must be

a stimulating color, usually a saturated hue or strong tint which is viewed, then removed from the field of vision and

a separate, distanced achromatic surface onto which the eye then projects the complement.

Afterimage requires a stronger hue stimulus than simultaneous contrast. Simultaneous contrast will occur even with quite muted colors, but it's almost impossible to generate an afterimage without strong, saturated color or brilliant tint as the stimulus.[12] Afterimage is also called successive contrast.

Contrast reversal is a variation of afterimage. In contrast reversal, a ghost image of the stimulating color appears as a complementary negative. For example, the eye may be stimulated with bright yellow diamonds on a white page. When the page is removed and a white blank paper is substituted, pale violet diamond forms will be seen where the yellow diamonds were and the white spaces between them will seem to be yellow.

. . . .

[12] It has been said that black and white do not create afterimages, but it's easily demonstrated that they do. The afterimage generated by black and white is a negative like a photographic negative. It has little relevance to color study.

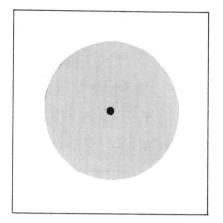 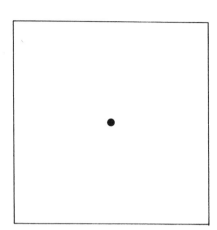

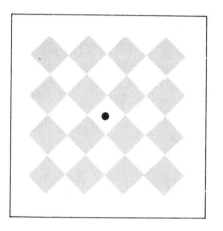 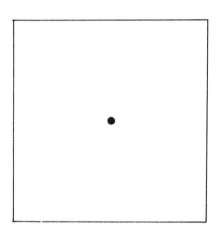

Figure 5–3 *Afterimage and Contrast Reversal.* These effects can be demonstrated by creating color cards about 12″ square. Make one with a large red circle; the other with yellow diamonds. Put a black dot into the center of a separate white page. Try each effect separately. Stare at the red circle as long as possible without blinking. Then blink once and look quickly at the white page with the black dot. Repeat the exercise with the yellow diamonds.

Complementary Contrast

Simultaneous contrast, afterimage, and contrast reversal occur when only one hue is present. Complementary contrast is a phenomenon closely related to simultaneous contrast. When colors containing any complementary contrast at all are placed against each other, that complementary relationship will be emphasized. A blue-green sample placed on red will appear more green. The same blue-green on orange will appear more blue.

Colors with a complementary relationship don't have to be saturated for that contrast to be emphasized. Nearly achromatic samples, with the slightest degree of complementary contrast, placed together will appear both more chromatic and more intensely different from each other. If a rose-gray is placed next to green-gray, each will appear to be more chromatic—a much redder rose-gray, a much greener green-gray. (See Figure C–16.)

Simultaneous contrast and complementary contrast are so closely related that it's sometimes hard to tell which is taking place. Few achromatics are wholly based on a mix of black and white. Some grays have a tendency to read as blue-gray; others have an orange or brown overtone. So-called neutral beiges have a warm overtone; neutral "putty" has a greenish overtone. Often when we think we are seeing simultaneous contrast we are really seeing complementary contrast—the eye reinforcing a tiny complementary relationship that already exists.

Tertiary Colors: Muted Hues and Brown

Tertiary colors are an enormous, almost limitless class of colors. Tertiary means "of the third rank," and tertiary colors are defined as "gray or brown, a mixture of two secondaries" (*The Random House Dictionary of the English Language* 1967). Any mixture of two secondaries, of course, also means a mixture of all primaries. (See Figure C–11.) Tertiary colors are a sort of color soup containing all possible hue ingredients with none apparent or dominating, although it should be possible for a trained eye to identify one or more of the hue ingredients.

A color dulled by the addition of its complement and retaining its hue identity is a muted hue, not a tertiary color. Red dulled by the addition of a little green is still red. Tertiary colors are chromatic neutrals, neither an identifiable hue nor a mix of black and white. Brown is a word often used to describe many of the colors in this "not black, gray, or identifiable-color" family.[13] Brown is not a hue. We say "brown" instead of "tertiary color" because it's common usage and equally descriptive. Colors aren't more or less brown, but browns may be more or less red, green, orange, and so forth.

Achromatic: True Grays and Theoretical Gray

A sample that has no discernible hue is called achromatic. True grays are a mixture of black and white. True grays may appear at first to be completely achromatic, but because colorants are imperfect there are chromatic overtones in every sample. Overtones can be "cool" (blue, violet, or green overtone) or "warm" (brown, red, or orange overtone). Sometimes the overtones are distinct; other times coolness or warmth or even a specific hue is detectable only when the sample is compared to a different gray. When warm grays and cool ones are placed next to each other, complementary contrast makes differences between them instantly visible.

. . . .

[13]Brown frequently has a heavy warm hue (red or orange) content rather than a cool one.

Theoretical gray is a concept used by color theorists to describe the imaginary perfect tertiary color—one of no detectable hue. Theoretical gray would be created by the mixture of all three primaries or, said another way, by the mixture of complementary colors. All of the limitations of light, viewer, and colorants keep theoretical gray a concept, not a reality. If colorants were perfect and illustration of theoretical gray was possible, there would be an identical achromatic result when violet and yellow, or red and green, or blue and orange were mixed. Visual logic doesn't allow us to imagine the middle mix of each of these pairs as the same. Whether the middle interval between complements is illustrated with paints, color papers, or just with imagination, each pair yields a distinctly different tertiary color. Seeing color with visual logic means that the middle mix of orange and blue will not be the same as that for violet and yellow. Theoretical gray is very much theoretical, very little gray.

Value

Value means relative light and dark in a sample. Value contrast exists whether or not hue is present. Hue is circular and continuous, but value is linear and progressive. A series of intervals of value, called a value scale, has a clear beginning and end. Value is first and most easily understood in achromatic form without the presence of hue.

Black is the lowest possible value.

White is the highest possible value.

Middle gray, the visual point exactly between black and white, is a middle or medium value, neither dark nor light.

A value scale appears at first to be a series of steps that are equal to each other. But in even intervals of value, each step is half as dark as the one after it and twice as dark as the one before it so the curve from light to dark increases in ever-doubling steps.[14]

Figure 5–4 *Value*. Value moves from dark to light whether or not hue is present.

. . . .

[14]Nineteenth-century studies in perception by Gustav Fechner and his predecessor E. H. Weber suggest that we perceive even intervals of value not as a mathematical progression (1,2,3,4,5,6, etc.) but as a geometric progression of ever-doubling steps (1,2,4,8,16,32, etc.). Each interval of value in a series is twice as dark as the one before and half as dark as the one following.

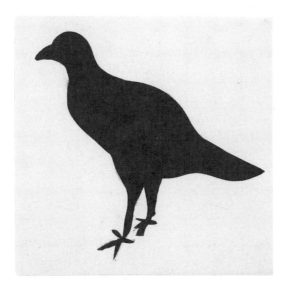

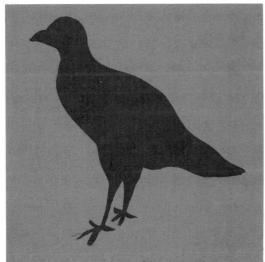

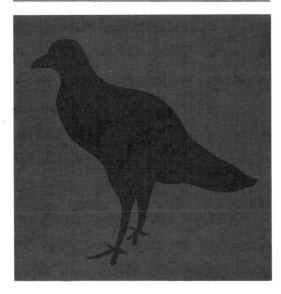

Figure 5–5 *Value and Image.*
Only difference in value between
a figure and its background
makes it visible. When the value
of the figure and the ground are
similar the image is hard to see.

Value and Image

Only value contrast makes objects distinguishable from their background. Hue and saturation have almost no role in "readability." Black and white drawings, the printed page, and film images are perfectly clear without hue. People with one of the many forms of color-blindness are nonetheless functional in a seeing world because color-blind really means "hue-blind," and hue is not a factor in the perception of image.

Contrast of light and dark determines the strength or graphic quality of an image. Black and white—the extremes of value contrast—create the strongest images. When value contrast is very slight, it's difficult to see an image. When there's no value contrast, there's no visible image at all. Discriminating relative light and dark in achromatic samples is reasonably easy. Occasionally it's difficult to make a judgment when trying to decide which of two very close grays is lighter or darker, but this is caused by the limitations of vision.

Transposing Image

All images (black and white or chromatic) are created by the placement of different values relative to each other within a composition. Even when shapes or forms within a composition remain identical, scrambling the value relationships creates a different image. (See Figure C–10.) A design may be printed in four values of gray on a white ground. To duplicate the image in values of a single hue or in multicolor, the new colors must maintain the same light-to-dark relationships and placements as those of the original design.

Pure Hues and Value

The most casual look at the spectrum reveals immediately that the saturated colors are at different levels of value.

Value is associated with the idea of luminosity—the light—reflecting quality of a color. Luminous hues reflect light, appear light, and are high in value. Nonluminous hues absorb light, are dark, and are low in value. Schopenhauer proposed a luminosity scale for each of Goethe's six saturated colors. He assigned a light-reflectance number value to each relative to the others (Albers 1963, 43):

RED	ORANGE	YELLOW	GREEN	BLUE	VIOLET
6	8	9	6	4	3

Yellow, the most luminous, is assigned 9, the highest number. Violet is assigned 3 and is the darkest of the pure colors. Red and green are

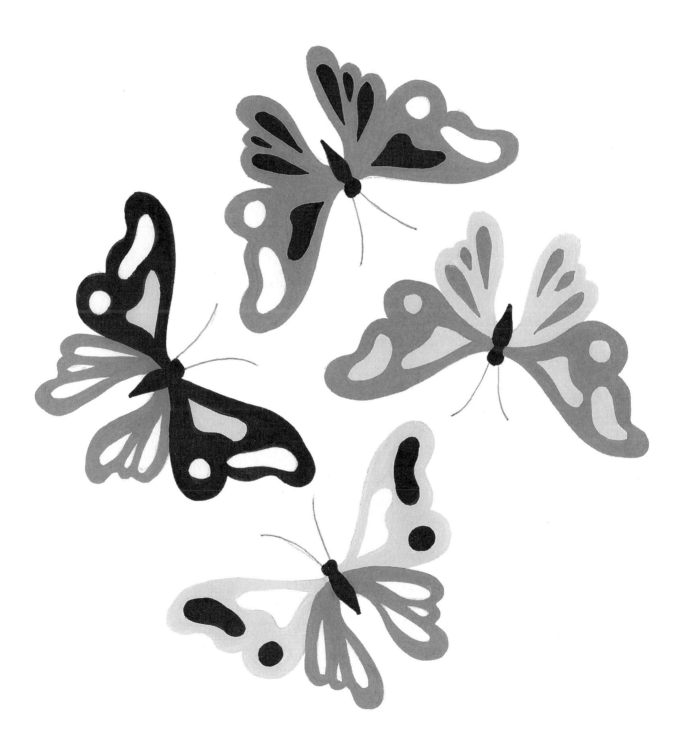

Figure 5–6 *Value and Image.* All the butterflies are identical in outline, but varying the placement of values within each makes each look different.

equal in value; blue and orange are placed relative to the others. Goethe's color circle was proposed as equal arcs of color, but Schopenhauer's modification created a color circle in which each arc of color was a different size. This circle of unequal arcs became the basis for one of the major mathematical concepts of color harmony.[15]

Tints and Shades

Colors are rarely used at full saturation; they are nearly always diluted in one or more ways. The simplest way to dilute pure colors is to change their value by adding black or white. (See Figure C–9.) Dilution of a pure color with white yields a *tint*. Tints retain the hue and add light-reflectance. Addition of a small amount of white yields a strong tint, often resulting in a color described as brilliant. Addition of a great deal of white reduces hues to tints that are extremely light-reflecting but barely identifiable as hues. Because of their light-reflecting quality, strong tints can be more intense color experiences than the saturated hues from which they derive. Violet, the darkest of the pure hues, appears more chromatic when white is added; the same can sometimes be said of blue, green, and red. No matter how hue-intense a tint may seem, it is a diluted hue and no longer a saturated color.

Dilution of a pure hue with black yields a *shade*.[16] Black absorbs all wavelengths of light so shades are reduced hue experiences. Black mutes the hue, dulling as well as darkening it. The range of shades may seem less familiar than tints, but it's just as extensive. Hue or chroma can be detected in a sample that appears to be entirely black by placing it next to a sample of a different black. Simultaneous contrast or complementary contrast will make the presence of hue immediately apparent. Unlike hues that are slightly tinted, slightly shaded hues are rarely mistaken for saturated colors.

Tone

There's no satisfactory definition in the color vocabulary for the noun *"tone."* *The Random House Dictionary of the English Language* (1967) gives it three consecutive and contradictory meanings. First, it's defined as a

. . . .

[15]Itten attributes this number concept to Goethe (Itten 1961 and 1970), but it does not appear in Goethe's *Color Theory*. It seems likely that Albers' attribution is correct.

[16]The word shade is often popularly misused to mean hue as in "that shade of red is more orange than this one." Shade is a word about value. It describes a color sample containing a hue and black.

pure color diluted by black or white (a tint or shade). The second definition states that tone is one hue modified by another (as "this is a blue tone, that's a greener one"). The third meaning is that a tone is a hue muted by gray. Each definition means a modification of hue, but each means a different kind of modification of hue.

One word can't mean variation in value, hue, and saturation interchangeably. If the word tone is to be used at all, it requires more descriptive support (a darker tone, a bluer tone, a grayer tone) to make its meaning known. Used in this way, tone becomes a synonym for "object" or "sample." To refer to a bluer tone, a muted tone, or a darker tone implies comparison with other tones and samples. Tone is clearest in meaning as a verb, part of the phrase "tone down." To "tone down" a hue means to mute it, to reduce its saturation. No one ever says "tone up" in reference to color.

Monochromatic Value Scales

A single hue illustrated in intervals of tints and shades is a monochromatic value scale. Only one hue is present. (See Figure C–9.) Monochromatic color schemes contain only one hue, but may have that hue in any number of values. The pure hue may be present in the grouping or it may be left out. Monochromatic value scales are easy to understand and to illustrate. Like the black-gray-white value scale, the only difficulty might be in discerning differences in close intervals of value.

Value and Hue Affinity

No one seems to have difficulty imagining or illustrating tints in any of the pure colors. The dilution of any color with white makes it more light-reflecting and more visible. At the same time, diluting the saturation with white makes that color less stimulating and therefore less tiring to the eye. Because saturated yellow is so much the lightest hue, intervals between it and other hues will also have great differences in value. The most common error in illustrating tints of hues that *contain* yellow (greens and oranges) is to render them as if they were diluted with yellow rather than with white. A tint retains its hue identity as it becomes lighter when white is added. Adding yellow to a green or an orange changes its value, but at the same time changes its hue.

Understanding and illustrating shades is a little more difficult. Many people find it particularly difficult to associate yellows and oranges with their shades. It is harder to imagine combinations of yellow and orange with black because the essential nature of yellow is highly luminous—the opposite of dark. But like all other hues, yellow and orange can be illustrated in the full range of values from near-white to near-black.

Comparing Value in Different Hues

Deciding which of two achromatic samples is lighter or darker is not very difficult. Deciding which of two samples of a single hue is lighter or darker is equally straightforward. Determining relative light and dark between two samples becomes difficult when the samples are different hues. It is more difficult when comparing warm and cool hues and most difficult when the hues are complementary.

Many color study problems call for determining *equal* value in different hues. This is one of the hardest of all color discriminations to make, particularly between complements. Only saturated red and green start as equal in value. For other pure hues to be made equal in value to each other, one must be made darker or lighter. Adding a great deal of black to yellow can make it as dark as violet. Adding a great deal of white to violet can make it as light as yellow. (See Figure C–9.)

A homemade viewing paper isolates any two samples to be compared and makes the job easier.

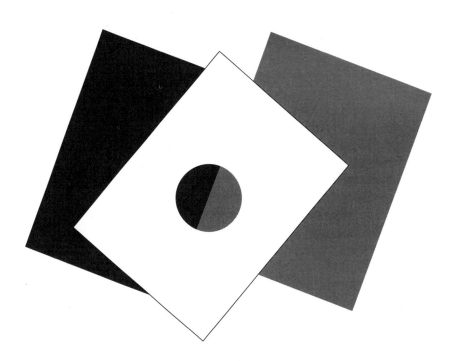

Figure 5–7 *A Viewing Paper.* Any stiff piece of white paper with a hole cut in it makes a good viewing paper. Use it to isolate sample colors for comparison.

The spectrum can be illustrated as a chart showing six hues in equal intervals of equal value. Each horizontal line shows six hues equal in value; each vertical is a single hue in equal intervals of value. (See Figure C–9.)

The chart can be in any number of steps, but it's most easily illustrated with between five, seven, or nine steps. Since pure hues don't exist as tidy intervals of value, a chart of six hues in a limited number of intervals of value is possible only if some hues appear as tints or shades, but don't appear on the chart as saturated color.[17]

Saturation

Dilution of a saturated color by black or white causes a change in value or light reflectance. Value is also called *light intensity*. The final descriptive quality of color—*saturation*—refers to changes in hue intensity or the contrast between dull and vivid. Satur*ated* color is color at its fullest expression of hue. Satur*ation* is a comparative term. A saturated color is a color at maximum chroma. When saturation is reduced, a color may retain its hue identity—retain its value—but be less vivid. Two red samples may be the same value, but one can be vivid and the other muted or dulled. As long as a sample retains its principal hue identity, it is a muted or dulled hue. When the sample loses its identity as a hue, it's a tertiary color. (See Figure C–11.)[18]

Brilliance is sometimes used as a synonym for saturation. Brilliance in common usage also describes strong, clear, light-reflecting tints. Red-violet diluted by a little white will make a color more brilliant than red-violet, but it's not a saturated color. Hues diluted by white may be brilliant, but they are not saturated. If a synonym for saturation is needed, hue intensity is a precise one.

Diluting Pure Hues with Gray

One way to change the hue intensity or saturation of a hue, without changing value, is by dilution with a gray that is equal in value to the pure color. When a sample of pure orange is placed next to a gray of equal value, the gray and the orange may become the parents in a parent-descendant color mixture. The midpoint between the gray and the orange, "gray-orange" will not be lighter or darker than its parent colors. It will be a muted hue, duller than the pure orange and more vivid (more chromatic) than the pure gray. Any pure hue can be diluted in this way. The gray/hue combination doesn't have to be a midpoint between the two. Hues can be grayed very slightly or a great deal and still retain their hue identity. (See Figure C–12.)

Diluting Pure Hues with the Complement

A second way to reduce saturation in a pure color is by adding the complement. Adding the complement reduces saturation in two ways.

. . . .

[17]Students determined to make a chart containing all the pure hues can do so by including a great number of intervals of value or by adjusting some of the pure colors.

Chroma is reduced (hue is muted) and value is reduced (the sample loses light). Muting colors by adding the complement results in the whole range of colors from muted hues to tertiaries. In mixing actual colorants, the addition of the complement to reduce saturation and/or to darken is the classic method in almost all media. When a pure color is diluted by even a small amount of its complement, it loses light because more wavelengths are absorbed by the mix. In colorant mixing, pure color will be muted and almost invariably made darker by the addition of a complement. (See Figure C–11.)

Colors diluted by the complement are much more a part of our visual experience than colors muted by the addition of gray. The natural world is a chromatic experience, not a black and white one. Pure black and white are rare in nature. Itten points out that "Nature shows such mixed colors very elegantly" (Itten 1970, 50) when green fruits ripen to red or leaves turn from green to brilliant red in the fall.

It's important to be reminded that the progression of steps between complements isn't necessarily parallel to paint-mixing results. For example, when steps between yellow and violet are determined visually, the violet immediately becomes muted and grayed, but also lighter as the two complements move to their achromatic center. In mixing actual colorants, the violet might darken as the mixture absorbs more wavelengths of light, or the opposite might happen, the yellow colorant might lighten it. The result would depend on the mixing qualities of the medium.

References

Albers, Josef. 1963. *Interaction of Color*. New Haven, Connecticut: Yale University Press.

Itten, Johannes. 1961. *The Art of Color*. Translated by Ernst Van Haagen. New York: Van Nostrand Reinhold.

Itten, Johannes. 1970. *The Elements of Color*. Edited by Faber Birren. Translated by Ernst Van Haagen. New York: Van Nostrand Reinhold.

Ostwald, Wilhelm. 1969. *The Color Primer*. New York: Van Nostrand Reinhold.

The Random House Dictionary of the English Language. 1967. Editor in Chief Jess Stein. New York: Random House, Inc.

. . . .

[18]A classic situation for an argument set off by differences in visual acuity and in concepts of colors: one man's brown is another man's burnt orange.

C h a p t e r **6**

Using Color

Art and Design

Art can be anything from a Toulouse-Lautrec poster to wrapping plastic around the California coast. Art is limited only by human imagination and the limitations of media and space. *Design* is applied art. It begins with a functioning product. Beauty may be inherent in that product, but many times it must be added. In the best designs, aesthetics and function are seamlessly integrated. Color creates the first impression whether the product is an office tower or a gum wrapper. "Black Rock" is the nickname for the CBS corporate headquarters in New York. The skyscraper would have a very different impact if its nickname were "Pink Rock."

Design and Color Perception

Everything we see and use has a design, from a dinner plate to a soap box and from a dress to a lamp post. Color is only one element of design. The other elements of design interact with color to create, alter, and reinforce color effects.

It's easy to think of using color as if design were a coloring book; just fill in the outlines with one group of colors for one effect and another group of colors for a different effect. This suggests that color modifies design and certainly this is true. The opposite is equally true—design modifies color. Design modifies color perception in such powerful ways that the two are inextricably combined. Before examining the ways in which colors can be manipulated to produce different effects, it's a good idea to review some of the other elements of design that impact on the perception of color.

Composition

A *composition* is a complete entity—something meant to be sensed as a whole. Composition includes the idea of arrangement (or relative placement) of elements within the whole. The word design is often used alone to mean design composition. Composition may be fluid or rigid, studied or accidental. Fallen leaves on the grass or wind on sand dunes may form beautiful compositions. For design professionals the process is deliberate—the product a result of a human mind, eye, and hand.

Intriciate compositions are constructed of smaller ones. A symphony is a musical composition conceived by a composer to be played as a whole, but each movement in a symphony has completeness and life of its own. Within each movement, single passages or melodies may be distinct compositions. Single notes within melodies have individual power and beauty. Compositions may be two- or three-dimensional. The surface of a sculpture has a beginning and an end as do garments, paintings, landscapes, or labels on perfume bottles. Each is a complete composition.

Color Composition

Color exists only in the context of something else. It describes or modifies tangible things (blue suede shoes) and intangible ones (the blue sky). Color is always part of a composition whether that composition is planned or accidental, devised or natural. Colors used together create a color composition. A group of colors selected for use together is called, depending on the design discipline or industry, a *palette*, a *colorway*, a *color story*, or some other collective term. Establishing a palette can be a first step in creating a design or a sort of after-the-fact summary. A palette alone can never substitute for the completed, colored design. The placement of colors relative to each other has a profound effect on the way each single color is perceived.

Limits and Borders

The limit of any composition—the place where it stops—is its visually logical edge. The limits of a composition may be as confined as the edges of a canvas or as immense as the edge of the horizon. Borders are an arbitrary device for establishing the limits of a design. Borders, like picture frames, enclose a composition and define what's within the composition and what is outside of it.

Ground and Carried Colors

The background of a color composition is called the *ground*. The colors laid against the ground are called *carried colors*. Ground establishes the visual reference point for carried colors. Different industries use different words for grounds. Colors printed on fabric or wall covering are said to be printed on a *ground,* but the background of a carpet or flag design is called the *field*. The paper for printed material is called *stock*. A printer may ask if he will be printing on "white stock or blue stock." No matter what each industry calls the ground or its material, "ground" means the background when color relationships are being discussed. Ground is one of the strongest modifiers of carried colors; changing a ground color in any way may change the effect of carried colors.

Ground is established by composition, not by color or relative area. It doesn't have to be the largest area in a composition. Carried color or design may cover substantially more area than ground. Visual clues and arrangement (composition) establish which area is image and which is ground.

Ordinarily a ground is thought of as part of a two-dimensional composition, but background exists for all things. A white house seen against green trees is white against a green ground; clouds are white against the blue ground of the sky. Even the sky is limited, where it stops against a horizon line of land or sea. Colors are seen only against a ground.

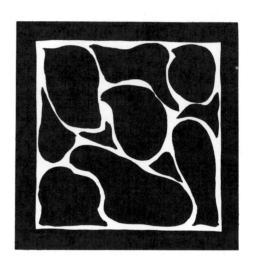

Figure 6–1 *Ground and Carried Color*. Composition, not area, determines what we perceive as ground and what we perceive as carried color. This black-bordered composition has very little white relative to black, but the white is the ground and the black is the carried color. In this illustration the black blobs are the image; white is the negative space.

In some designs it's difficult or impossible to distinguish between ground and carried colors. Is a zebra black with white stripes or white with black stripes? A checkerboard with equal blocks of different colors or a striped textile has no defined ground. Uncertainty about which part of a design is the ground and which part the carried colors doesn't lessen the effects that colors in a composition have upon each other. Creating a design in which the ground is ambiguous can be a deliberate choice. Whenever colors are placed against or on top of each other, interactions of ground and carried colors will occur.

Ground and Graphic Quality

White grounds give sharpness and clarity to any design even if the carried colors are muted colors or tints. Black grounds provide a strong contrast particularly behind light colors, but nothing is comparable in sparkle and crispness to the effect produced by colors on a white ground. (See Figure C–20.)

Reducing value contrast between a ground and its carried colors softens and mutes a color composition as a whole. It makes no difference whether the ground or carried colors are achromatic, brilliant hues, or some of each. The closer the ground and carried colors are in value, the less graphic the image will be. Strong graphic images and high contrast are not always desirable. An image can be too contrasting in practical ways. Superhighway signs are dark green and off-white because they have been demonstrated to produce a lower level of glare, and therefore eye fatigue, than black and white ones.

When a ground and carried colors are close in value, the overall effect can be lifeless and flat. The flatness can be offset (without disrupting the color composition as a whole) by the introduction of dark lines or small patches of white highlights into the design. No matter how proportionally small the quantity of white may be or what its placement, it will give sparkle to the rest of the composition. Black or dark lines or patches are also effective in providing contrast.

Negative Space

Negative space is the area in a two- or three-dimensional composition that is outside a design or image. It's the "unfilled" area around and sometimes within the design. Negative space is often but not always the same area as the ground. The negative spaces and the images or patterns in color compositions have equal power to alter the way colors are seen.

Line and Mass

As long as there is value contrast between a block of color and its ground, an image will be distinct. Differences between areas may be intensified by contrasts of hue or saturation, but only differences in value create a visible "edge" between masses of color. Line is a thin, elongated area of color that contrasts in value with a ground. A line has

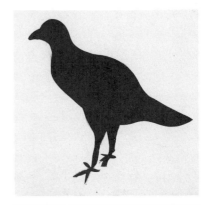

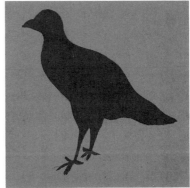

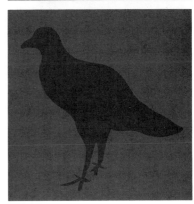

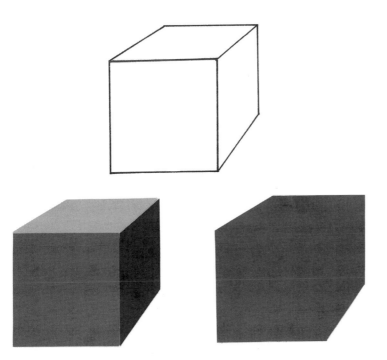

Figure 6–2 (Above) *Graphic Quality.* The closer in value carried colors are to their ground, the more muted the image. Contrast of value between ground and carried colors controls "readability" of an image.

Figure 6–3 (Left) *Line and Mass.* The same figure can be illustrated using line, mass, or a combination of both (not shown).

length without breadth. There are thick lines and thin ones and colored and broken lines, but they have one common attribute—great length in relation to little width. An enclosed or nearly-enclosed line drawn on a page separates an image from the ground. Line has tremendous visual power, much greater than its weight or area. A block of one color laid against a ground of another with the same or similar value is difficult to distinguish, but the thinnest line between them creates a clear separation. We think of line as being dark or black, but it can be any value. The greater the contrast in value between line and ground, the more strongly we sense separation between the image and the ground. Black line on a white page creates a strong image, dark gray line a weaker one, and pale gray line hardly any image at all.

Almost all special effects of color result from juxtaposed color masses without the intervention of line. Among these special effects are optical mixes, vanishing boundaries, fluting, transparence illusion, and vibration. Each of these relies on blocks of color-laid-on color alone. Adding value-contrasting line between blocks of color reduces or eliminates color illusions and special effects.

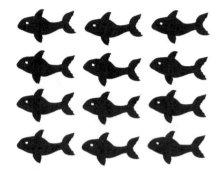

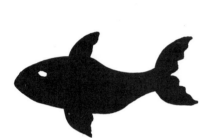

Viewing Distance, Image, and Pattern

There's always a range of distance from which a design will ordinarily be seen. Designing graphics for the telephone book assumes a close reading distance. Designing wallpaper presupposes a middle distance; highway billboards another viewpoint entirely. Whether a design is seen as image, pattern, or texture depends on composition and reading distance, not on the actual size of the design elements.

A design motif can be a single figure enclosed by line, a color mass, or a combination of both. A single motif seen against a ground is an image. It can be representational or nonrepresentational—a camel or a raggedy-edged blob. The size of the image is unimportant. What's definitive about an image is that it is sensed as one element against a ground. An image repeated against a ground is a pattern. A pattern can be regular or random, geometric or fluid. Pattern is sensed as a whole, but individual motifs can be distinguished.

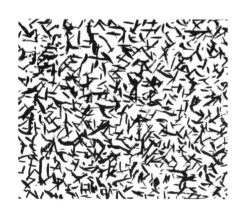

Figure 6–4 *Image, Pattern, and Texture.* Scale and arrangement determine whether we see the fish as an image (center), a pattern (many fish, top), or a texture (fish that are too small to see, bottom).

Optical Mixes

There's a point at which multiple motifs become too small and closely spaced to be seen as pattern. Optical mixes result when masses of color too small to be perceived as separate elements converge to create the effect of an entirely new color. There is no distinguishable ground or carried color in an optical mix; the colors fuse in the eye to create a single new color. Optical mixes can be made of two or many colors. Photo-offset printing uses optical mixes entirely to reproduce images in black and white or color. Dots of ink too small to be seen individually without a magnifying glass merge to produce the printed image. Optical mixing was used by the Impressionists to create shadow and effects of dimension without mixing paints on the palette. Seurat called his optical mixing "divisionism" (Hope 1990).[1] In divisionism, the colors on the canvas were pure colors or tints laid on in tiny dots. (Impressionism is a word coined from the name of a Monet painting.)

Complements combined will appear muted or shadowed. Hues other than complements will combine to form a new hue. Because optical mixes are combined colors, the qualities present in those colors affects the outcome. If the colors contrast in value (and almost all do), the resulting surface will appear to have texture. An optical mix of yellow, which is light, and red, which is darker, will produce a broken and somewhat rough orange surface. Combining analogous hues of similar value produces an enormously lively surface. Each color acts as if it were the ground for the other. Differences are emphasized, but they are too small to be perceived as separate masses. Anything covered with tiny patches of close colors dances with a surface energy and life not possible with a single color.

Vibration

When blocks of saturated complementary or near-complementary colors are placed next to or on top of one another, the colors seem to vibrate. This kind of complementary-contrast vibration is caused by the eye's response to more than one intense hue stimulus. The eye seeks equilibrium in opposite, contradictory ways at the same time. Strong, clear tints of complements will generate the same reaction. Muted colors and shades don't stimulate the eye in the same way. (See Figure C–14.) The discomfort caused by this kind of hue-vibration is aggravated when the contrasting hues are equal in value. Without value contrast between blocks of color it's difficult to see the edge between them. The struggle to focus on edge, added to the struggle to reach equilibrium, ends in a completely miserable visual experience. Value-contrasting line introduced between blocks of color reduces or eliminates this kind of vibration.

A different kind of vibration results from poor design scale in a pattern relative to its viewing distance. A pattern is a repeated design motif. When motifs in a pattern are just smaller than can be comfortably discriminated individually, but slightly too large to merge into texture, the eye makes repeated attempts to focus. It holds the images briefly, then must refocus. Hue isn't necessary; vibration resulting from

. . . .

[1]His style of painting is now better known as "pointillism."

poor design scale occurs as often in achromatic compositions as in chromatic ones.

Vibration can be initially exciting to the eye but it quickly becomes physically tiring. Aesthetic experiments like the "Op" (optical) art of the 1960s demonstrated the power of both scale and color in creating visually disturbing design. The intent and result of these works was to create a maximum of visual disorientation.

Vanishing Boundaries

Vanishing boundaries occur when blocks of close colors of equal value are next to each other. The blocks of color seem to merge and lose their edges. Vanishing boundaries are partly a function of an individual's threshold—the point of the single interval. As long as the colors are close in hue and close in value, the edges will merge to some extent. (See Figure C–13 .) Boundaries between colors can't vanish when colors are different in value or when a value-contrasting line lies between the blocks of color.

Spatial Effects of Colors

Color qualities determine whether we perceive objects as larger or smaller or as advancing or receding. Another way to describe "advance and recede" is to call it "near and far." Some colors have inherent qualities of "nearness" or "farness." Light blues will seem to move away; warm colors of any value close in. By manipulating hue, value, or saturation, surfaces and objects can be made to appear larger or smaller, or nearer or farther away than they really are.

The key phrase in understanding how colors will advance or recede relative to one another in hue and saturation is "all other factors being equal." (See Figure C–15.)

Hue: Warm colors will advance relative to cool ones. Your right foot in the red shoe looks larger than your left foot in the green shoe.

Saturation: More saturated colors will advance; more muted colors will recede. The pink elephant seems a lot bigger and closer than the gray one.

Value: Objects in light colors will appear larger than the same objects in dark colors. A white bear looks bigger and nearer than a black one standing in the same spot.

When both dark and light colors are laid against a ground and no hue or only one hue is present, the contrast of value between ground and carried colors determines which will appear closer. The color with more contrast in value against the ground will advance; the color closer in value to the ground will recede. Dark colors will advance relative to light colors on a light ground; lights advance relative to darks on a dark ground.

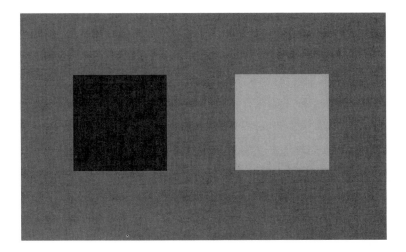

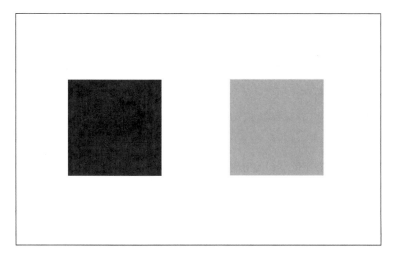

Figure 6–5 *Spatial Effect of Colors and Value.* The value contrast between a ground and its carried colors determines whether dark or light colors will seem to come forward. The color with the greater contrast to the ground will advance; the color closer in value to the ground will recede.

Combinations of colors in which "all other factors being equal" except one are rare. The dominant quality of a sample—its warmth, high value, or brilliance—determines whether it will seem to move forward or backward relative to other colors. In a gray world, yellow will bounce forward. In a black world, gray will glow with light.

Color and Area

Color and area relate to each other in two distinct ways. First, selecting a color from a small sample and applying it to a large surface or vice versa changes the impact of that color. Colors appear more chromatic when seen in a larger area. Light colors and dark ones are equal in this effect. Colors selected in a small chip and applied to a large plane will also change in apparent value. As a general rule, small areas of light or dark color will move toward closer to middle values when the area is increased.[2] A good illustration of this effect occurs when colors are selected to paint a house. A house is a large object and the chips for choosing house paint are very small. Paint the house with the darkest brown paint on a chart and it will appear medium brown. Charcoal gray, nearly black on the chart, will be a dusty medium-dark when applied. Pale yellow house paint is always more yellow than expected.

The second way in which area and color interact is in what Itten called "contrast of extension" (Itten 1970, 59). Contrast of extension is about the relative impact of colors when they are seen in larger and smaller areas. Albers had a succinct phrase for it: "Quantity is a quality" (Albers 1963, 43). This quality of contrast of extension or area is a part of visual impact and is discussed in Chapter 7.

Color Control: Placement and Change

Light is the first modifier of color perception. Colors change under different light sources because of an interaction between light source and the colorant. Changes in color caused by changes in light are almost impossible to predict or control in advance. The second cause of color change is the interaction between grounds and carried colors. These changes are caused by placement. Choice of ground color determines how carried colors will appear. The reverse can also be true; carried colors affect the way the ground is seen.[3] It's not particularly important that the ground and carried colors be clearly defined as such. As long as colors are laid one upon another, each will affect the other in predictable ways.

There are three ways in which the relationship of grounds to carried colors can cause change: simultaneous contrast, complementary contrast, and ground subtraction. The key word in all cases is "contains." Two ways are already familiar.

. . . .

[2]Under some circumstances the direction in which value changes to lighter or darker depends on the placement of the color relative to a light source. Floors in general will appear lighter and ceilings darker than a small sample of color in the hand.

[3]As an example, a neutral ground in a wallpaper with a red pattern will appear cool against the red but will appear warmer if the printed pattern is changed from red to blue.

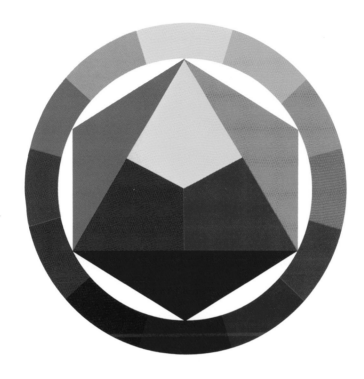

Figure C–1 *The Artists'* Spectrum.

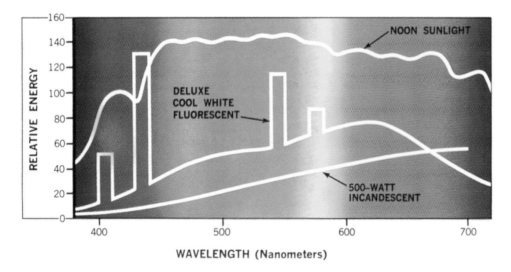

Figure C–2 *The Visible Wavelengths of Light.* Different light sources emit the various
wavelengths in different proportions. Each light source has a characteristic pattern
of energy at the various wavelengths. The white light that results will vary in warmth
(red-orange-yellow) or coolness (blue-green) as a result. Courtesy of General Electric.

Figure C–3 *Process Colors.*

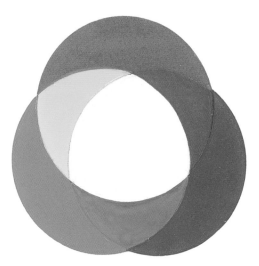

Figure C–4 *Additive Colors.* Red, green, and blue are the primary colors of light; yellow, magenta, and cyan are the secondary colors. When all colors are present they combine to yield white light.

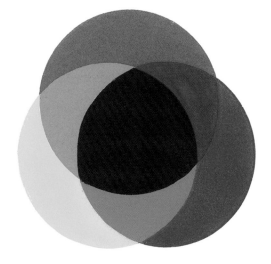

Figure C–5 *Subtractive Colors.* Red, yellow, and blue are the primary colors of the artists' spectrum; green, orange, and violet are the secondary colors. When the three primaries are combined in colorants, all light is absorbed and the result is a dark area of no perceptible hue.

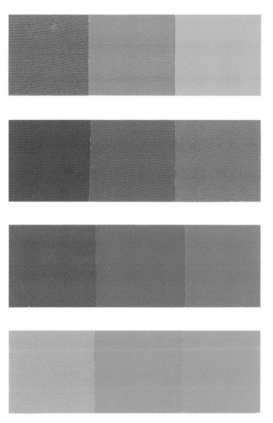

Figure C–6 *Analogous Colors.* Analogy is a quality of hue regardless of saturation or value. Saturated colors, muted colors, tints, and shades can be analogous.

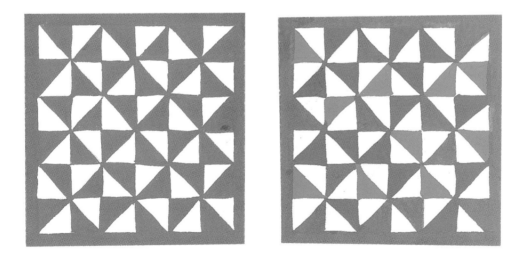

Figure C–7 *Color Harmony.* Analogy lends interest to simple designs as well as complex ones. The same quilt rendered in blue on white becomes livelier when the blue is varied with closely analogous blues and greens.

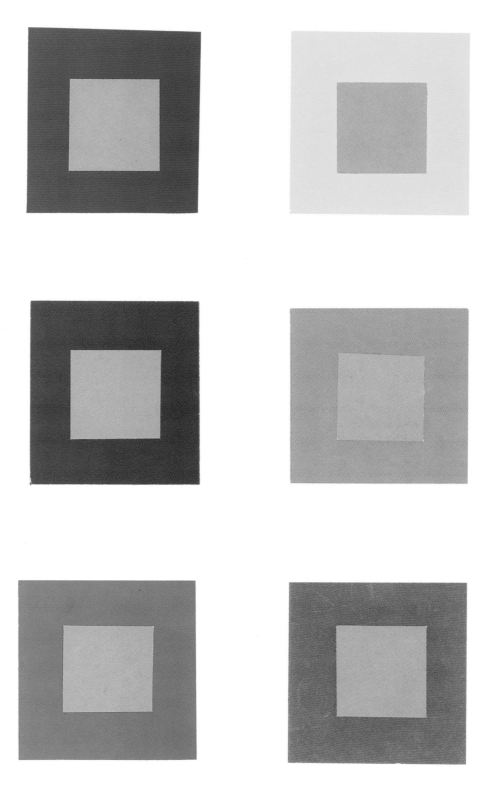

Figure C–8 *Simultaneous Contrast.* Study the gray square in the center of each pair of complements by staring at both as long as possible without blinking. Cover the other two sets as you look at each pair.

Figure C–9 *Six Hues in Even Intervals of Value.*

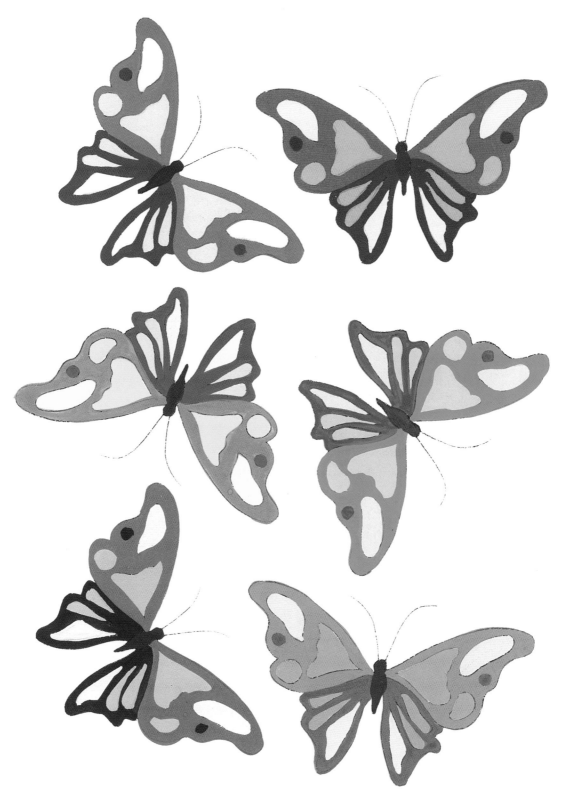

Figure C–10 *Maintaining Image.* Although the butterflies are different hues the value relationships are identical so they appear to be the different color versions of the same butterfly. (See Figure 5–6 for the opposite effect.)

Figure C–11 *Complementary Colors.* When a small amount of the complement is added to a saturated color, that color is muted but remains recognizable. When complements are mixed to their visual midpoint, the result is a chromatic neutral—a color of no discernible hue or tertiary color.

Figure C–12 *Pure Hues Diluted by Gray of Equal Value.* Even though the hues lose their hue-intensity, they remain the same in value.

Figure C–13 Vanishing Boundaries.

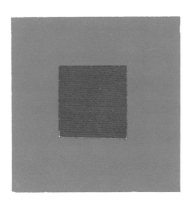
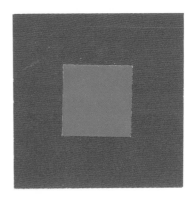

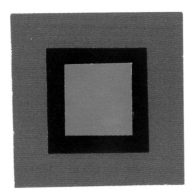

Figure C–14 *Vibration.* Vibration between colors can be reduced or eliminated by adding a value-contrasting mass or line.

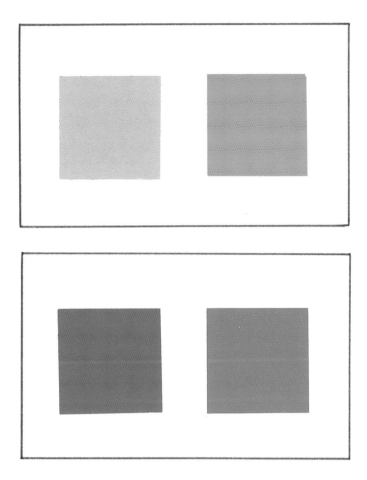

Figure C–15 *Spatial Effects of Colors.* When colors are equal in value, warm colors will advance relative to cool ones and more saturated colors will advance relative to muted ones.

Figure C–16 *Complementary Contrast.* Simultaneous contrast occurs even when only a suggestion of hue is present. Here, the same center square takes on opposite qualities when placed on gray-red and green.

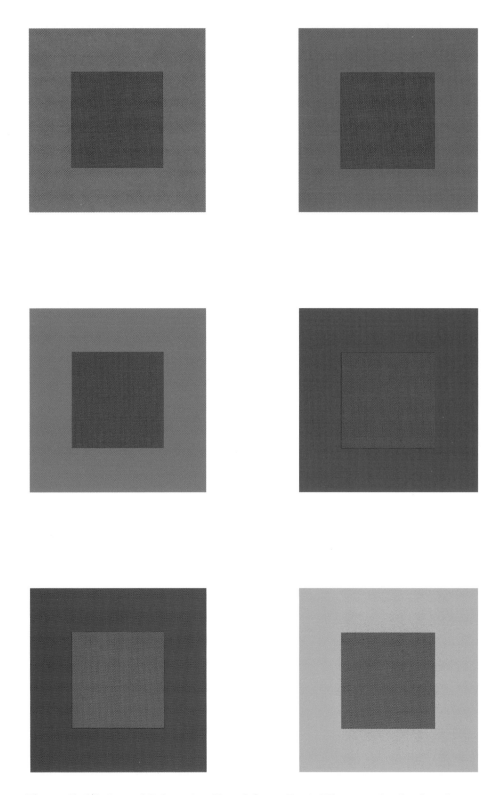

Figure C–17 *Ground Subtraction (One Color as Two).* When a color is placed on a ground that has some similar qualities, those common qualities will be reduced and differences between the two emphasized. A single color appears to be two different colors.

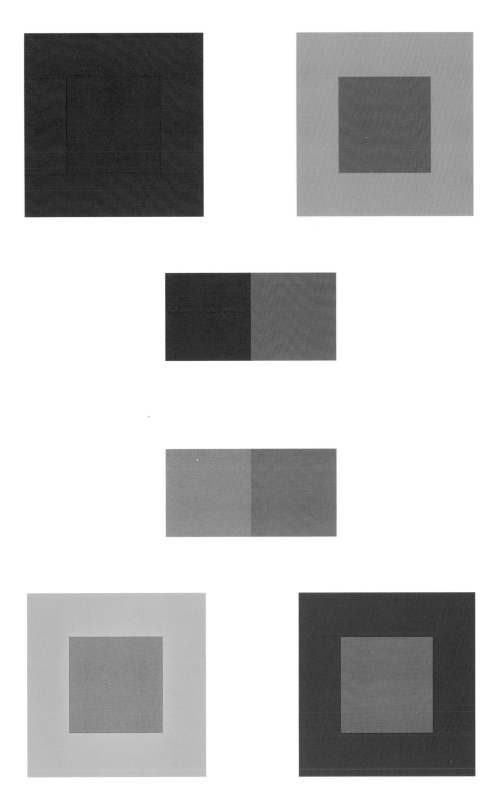

Figure C–18 *Ground Subtraction (Two Colors as One).* Ground can be manipulated so that two different colors appear to be the same.

Figure C–19 *Transparence Illusion.*

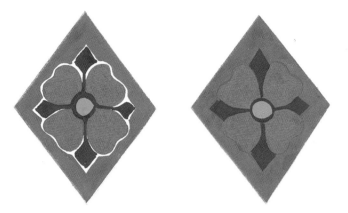

Figure C–20 *Different Hues of Similar Value in Composition.* Carried colors of similar value look lifeless and flat when there is no contrast in value with the ground. The smallest amount of value contrast enlivens the composition.

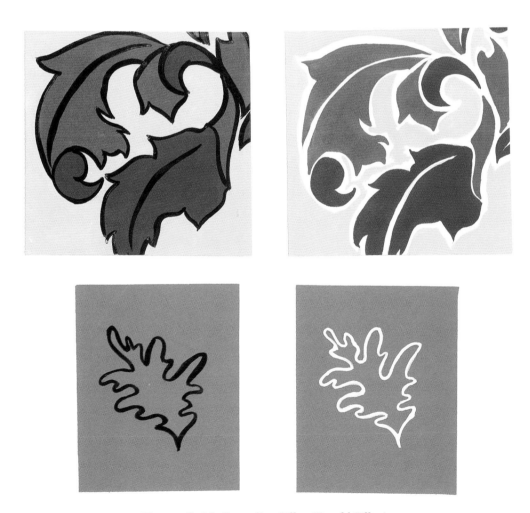

Figure C–21 *Spreading Effect (Bezold Effect).*

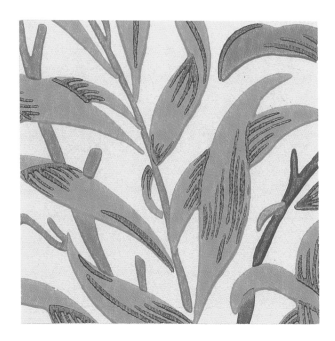

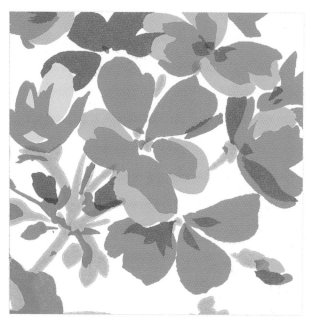

Figure C–22 *Color Harmony.* Above: A document nineteenth-century William Morris wallpaper accurately reproduces the beauty of the original palette. One muted hue is used in several values and a tertiary color (ground and stems) gives the muted hue more hue-intensity by contrast. Courtesy of Sanderson. Below: A contemporary wallpaper from Brunschwig and Fils illustrates the harmony of even intervals of value in pure colors and tints in a complementary relationship.

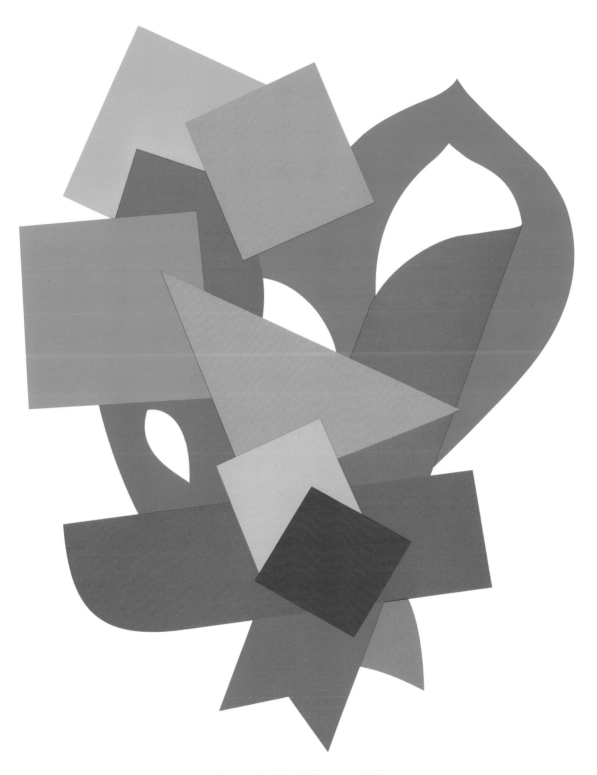

Figure C–23 *High Impact Colors.*

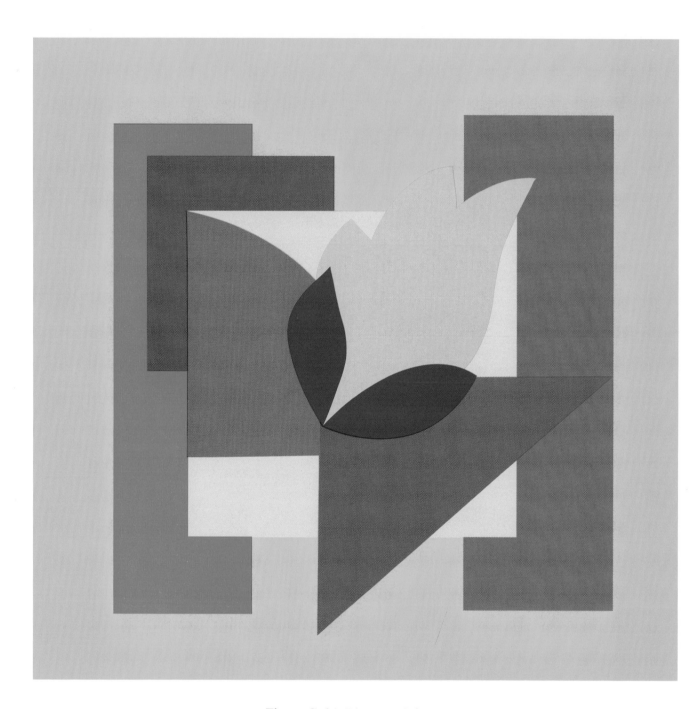

Figure C–24 *Dissonant Colors.*

Simultaneous Contrast: The ground or the carried color contains a single hue; the other is achromatic. The achromatic will take on qualities of the complement.

For example, a gray square on orange will seem blue-ish gray. The same gray square on blue will appear warmer and more orange-gray. (See Figure C–8.)

Complementary Contrast: The ground and the carried color contain hues that are complementary. Differences in hue, however slight, will be emphasized. (See Figure C–16.)

Imagine greenish-gray laid on rose beige. One contains a hint of green; the other a fraction of red. Used as ground and carried colors, they appear almost red and green.

Simultaneous contrast generates hue difference between samples when only one hue is actually present. Complementary contrast emphasizes differences between two samples that contain complementary, opposing hues. Each emphasizes differences between samples already unlike. Simultaneous contrast and complementary contrast are effects of hue alone.

Ground Subtraction

Ground subtraction is completely different. It intensifies the differences between colors which contain qualities in common. Ground subtraction affects hue, value, and saturation equally.

Any ground subtracts its own qualities from colors it carries. Common qualities of hue, value, or saturation will be reduced. The differences that remain will be emphasized. (See Figure C-20.)

One way to understand ground subtraction is to say that for every ground-and-carried-color combination there are three questions:

1. What qualities of hue, value, or saturation does each carried color have in common with its ground?

2. What is reduced?

3. What is left?

Ground subtraction can be demonstrated by selecting a middle interval between any two parent colors, cutting two small pieces of it, and placing one piece in the center of each parent color. For example, middle gray placed on black will appear lighter; its common blackness is reduced and whiteness intensified. The same middle gray on a white

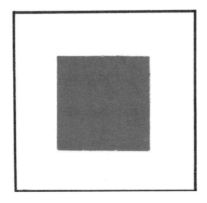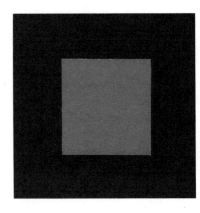

Figure 6–6 *Ground Subtraction.* The same gray is placed in the center of each square. A light ground reduces light in the carried color and makes it appear darker. A dark ground reduces the dark in a carried color and makes it appear lighter.

ground will appear darker; its whiteness is reduced and its blackness emphasized. Blue-green placed on blue will appear more green; the blue common to both will be reduced and the green remaining will be emphasized. Blue-green placed on green will appear more blue; the common green will be reduced and the blue intensified. A gray-green placed on gray will appear more green. Placed on green, it will appear grayer.

Some media, like silkscreen, limit the number of actual blocks of color in a design. Placing colors on different grounds within a design can create an illusion of more colors than are really present. The familiar illusion of ground subtraction is of a single color appearing to be two different ones by placing it on different grounds. The illusion can be reversed and two different colors made to appear to be the same by placing colors on different grounds that reduce specific qualities and reinforce others. (See Figure C–18.) For example, with a little manipulation of grounds and carried colors, a green and a yellow-green can be made to look as if they were exactly the same color. Yellow-green placed on yellow will appear more green because the common yellow is reduced. A "greener" green (containing less yellow) placed on a blue-green ground will appear more yellow because the blue that is common to both is reduced. The same technique used to create an illusion of identical hue can be used with value, saturation, or a combination of all three qualities of color.

Color Change and Design Practice

Whenever two colors are planned for use together there is a potential for change. This is true in the fashion industry for textiles, in graphic arts for print and paper colors, and in home furnishings for paint and carpet. Ground subtraction, simultaneous contrast, and complementary contrast have their most unexpected impact when colors are close to each other, not when they are very different. Even the most sophisticated designer has an unspoken expectation that similar colors will "work" together. Unfortunately, the more similar two colors are, the more apparent their differences will be when they are placed together. Color changes caused by simultaneous contrast, complementary contrast, and ground selection are constant and predictable. They influence every color composition. They are as much positive forces as they are effects to be prevented because unlike color changes caused by light, *changes caused by placement can be controlled by the designer from the earliest stages of a design.*

Influenced and Influencing Colors

Pure colors and strong tints are often considered to be more influencing and muted colors more influenced. This is true for afterimage, simultaneous contrast, and complementary contrast. More chromatic colors influence the more muted ones.

Afterimage depends entirely on a powerful hue stimulus. The most carefully contrived attempt at creating an afterimage with muted colors won't work because the eye is at rest and doesn't need to generate missing hues. Simultaneous contrast requires the presence of a single hue and an adjacent achromatic area. The more chromatic or brilliant the stimulating color, the stronger the effect will be on the achromatic one, but simultaneous contrast will occur whether or not that hue is highly saturated. Complementary contrast takes place when there is the slightest, most fractional complementary relationship between hues. A muted color that appears gray when seen alone will take on discernible hue when placed next to an equally muted color containing a hint of the opposite hue. (See Figure C–16.)

In ground subtraction, the saturation level of the ground has no special bearing on whether or not the ground will change a carried color. All qualities in a ground have equal power to effect change. The only requirement is that the ground and carried colors have one or more elements in common.

No carried color is exempt from the influence of its ground. An apparently pure primary red sample placed on very slightly different red grounds will appear more violet or more orange in contrast to those grounds. Complex mixed colors like tertiaries are more subject to change by placement, to be the "influenced" colors because the more elements a color contains, the more likely it is to have something in common with another color. Complex colors change more frequently because they have more opportunities to do so, but the changes aren't stronger than the ones that take place with simpler colors.

Maximum Effect in Color Change

Colors appear to change most when complementary contrast and ground subtraction (or simultaneous contrast and ground subtraction) are in force at the same time. This seems contradictory at first. How can colors be both alike and different? How can colors contain opposite and common qualities at the same time? Neutrals, "browns," and tertiaries are complex colors. They are hues diluted by complements, by black, white, or gray. The more elements a color contains, the more likely it is to have one or more qualities of hue, value, or saturation in common with its ground *and* others that are complementary to the ground.

Imagine a "brown" square, the middle mix of blue and orange, placed on an orange ground. The orange (common hue) in the brown will be reduced by ground subtraction. The blue contained in the brown will be intensified twice; first as the remainder after the orange is reduced, then by complementary contrast against its orange ground. The same brown square, placed on a blue ground, will look very much more orange as the blue is reduced and the orange intensified.

The first reason to identify placements that cause change is in order to avoid them. The more constructive reason is to be able to use them to enhance color effects. A colorist can use placement to intensify or mute color, to make lights darker, and darks lighter. Clever placement can expand the boundaries of media by making two or three colors look like four, five, or more.

Illusions

Color is the stuff of sorcery—almost anything done with it yields an illusion. We use simultaneous contrast, complementary contrast, ground subtraction, optical mixes, close and distant value intervals, and tricks of scale to achieve magical effects. Most color illusions depend on blocks of color-laid-on color. Adding line or open ground area between blocks of color eliminates many color illusions. Illusions rely on very specific arrangements of the blocks of color. Well-controlled intervals between colors are also crucial. Illusions are produced equally by color selection and by arrangement or placement of colors. Neither factor will work alone.

Transparency and Transparence Illusion

Transparency in color can be a fact. There are opaque liquids, like milkshakes, and transparent ones, like coffee. A gallon container of strawberry milkshake is the same color as a half cup. Transparent liquids appear stronger in hue as their volume increases, a phenomenon Josef Albers describes as "volume color" (Albers 1963, 45). In a

deep gallon container, the coffee is very dark. The coffee spilled in the
saucer is as light as tea.

Transparent media like colored inks allow light to pass through the
colorant and reflect back from white paper underneath. As layers of ink
are added, the transparency decreases (less light reflects back from the
underlying paper) and the covered areas become darker. These are
true transparencies, not illusions.

Some opaque colors have an apparently transparent nature. Cool
opaque colors, especially tints of blue and green, often seem transparent. Warm opaque colors, particularly those containing red, seem more
dense and opaque.

The illusion of transparency is astonishingly easy to generate in
opaque colors. Any parent-descendent color mixture (two colors and
the middle interval between them), arranged with parent colors cross-

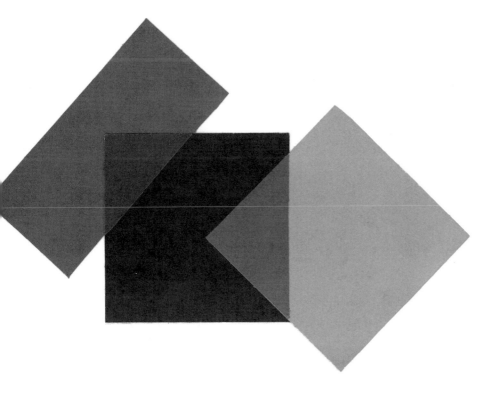

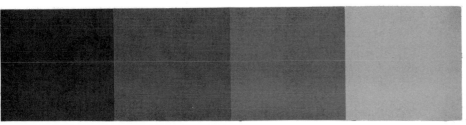

Figure 6–7 *Transparence Illusion.*
Placement of parent-descendant
intervals creates the illusion of
transparency. The same grays,
arranged in a strip, show no
effect of transparency.

ing one another and the middle interval in the area of overlap, will create a flawless illusion of transparency every time. (See Figure C–19.) One of the parent colors will always appear to be on top of the other in the overlap area. The "top" color is determined by the rules of spatial effects. Lighter colors advance (seem to be on top) relative to darker ones, warm colors advance relative to cool ones, brilliant colors advance relative to muted ones, and so on. Transparency illusion has no limits of hue, value, or saturation. Any color samples arranged as if they were crossing, with a visually logical interval between them in the overlap area, will create the illusion.

Texture

The impression of texture on a flat surface results from value contrast within an optical mix. *Optical mixes* occur when masses of color too small to be perceived as separate elements combine in the eye to create the effect of an entirely new color. Ground is "lost" visually in an optical mix. The surface is overlaid with the carried colors so completely that the colors, fused in the eye, become the ground. The eye reacts to very small masses of contrasting colors laid against each other according to the rules for spatial effects. Some colors will recede, some advance, and the surface will seem to dance with dimension. The higher the value contrast between the colors, the stronger the illusion of three-dimensional texture.

Fluting

Fluting is an illusion in which a series of vertical stripes of uniform width appear to have concavity, like the channels of a Doric column.[4] The fluted effect occurs when stripes are arranged in a series of even, progressive intervals of value. Each stripe reacts to its neighbor as if the neighbor were a ground. It appears lighter along the edge where it abuts its darker neighbor and darker along the edge where it abuts its lighter neighbor. Like the three bears' porridge, the stripes have to be just right. They can't be too wide or the eye won't take in both edges at the same time. They can't be too narrow or they will appear to be lines instead of vertical blocks of color. Spectrum colors arranged as stripes will appear fluted, but only because saturated colors are progressive in value. Stripes of the spectrum hues in which the values are equal won't appear fluted.

. . . .

[4]In wider stripes, the illusion is sometimes of convexity, but the effect is still called fluting.

Figure 6–8 *Fluting*. Fluting is an illusion that requires specific shapes and placement. The stripes must be set up in a progressive series of steps of value.

Spreading Effect

Wilhem von Bezold, a German physicist, described what is called "spreading effect" in 1876 (Goldstein 1984, 272). Spreading effect is different from most illusions because line, not mass, causes it. *Spreading effect* can occur in two ways. When a pattern or design of dark line is laid on a middle value ground (a hue or a gray) the ground itself will appear darker. If white or light line is substituted for the dark, the ground will appear lighter. The lightness or darkness of the line seems to "spread" into the ground. (See Figure C–21.) Spreading effect occurs in multi-color designs when areas or masses of color are separated from the ground by dark or light line. When the forms are enclosed by dark line, all colors appear darker. When forms are enclosed by light line, all colors appear lighter. The dark or light outline affects all colors in the composition.

Spreading effect, which depends on line, has an effect opposite to ground subtraction. If outlines thicken to the point where they become dark or light masses with carried colors on top of them, they are no longer outlines. They have become grounds. Darker grounds make middle values appear lighter; lighter grounds make them appear darker. Spreading effect in a multicolor composition happens only when design elements are outlined against a ground. Spreading effect is also called *Bezold Effect*. Another and less specific way that it is sometimes described is to say that the balance of a composition is changed by adding, removing, or changing one color only.[5]

References

Albers, Josef. 1963. *Interaction of Color*. New Haven, Connecticut: Yale University Press.

Goldstein, E. Bruce. 1984. *Sensation and Perception*. Belmont, California: Wadsworth Publishing Company.

Hope, Augustine and Walch, Margaret. 1990. *The Color Compendium*. New York: Van Nostrand Reinhold.

Itten, Johannes. 1970. *The Elements of Color*. Edited by Faber Birren. Translated by Ernst Van Haagen. New York: Van Nostrand Reinhold.

. . . .

[5]Some authorities say that the effect of the apparent shift in the ground color is not from dark to light, but from more blue to more yellow or vice versa.

Chapter

7

Color Harmony/
Color Effect

Color harmony means beauty or "pleasingness" in a group of colors. It refers to the collective impression of colors used together—the overall visual effect of a color composition. The search for laws of harmony in color combinations grew from the inquiry into natural phenomena that characterized the Enlightenment. There was an assumption that certain colors used together were inherently harmonious and the laws for them, like gravity, only awaited discovery. Artists and critics still explore the nature of color and beauty as abstract ideas, but designers have different concerns. The competitive edge of a "good" color combination can mean life or death in the marketplace. The search for laws of color harmony in the world of design is the search for marketable color combinations.

Johannes Itten characterized color harmony as "the joint effect of two or more colors" (Itten 1961, 21). Harmony means beauty, but beauty is only one possible outcome of combining colors. "The joint effect of two or more colors" is too comprehensive a phrase to confine to harmony. It must also encompass disturbing colorways whose impact is powerful and dissonant. More questions arise about any color grouping than "Is it pretty?" Is a combination startling or visually aggressive? Is it restful and soothing? Boring and monotonous? Does looking at it produce vertigo and a splitting headache? Will an image appear more or less powerful for having been rendered in certain colors?

"The *pleasing* joint effect of two or more colors" is more precisely what color harmony means. Unfortunately, the only rational standard for a pleasing combination of colors is that someone is pleased by it. Since almost everyone has different favorite colors or combinations of colors, the idea that a favorite combination might be aesthetically "unlawful" is absurd. This hasn't prevented color theorists from asserting it; Munsell used the work "admissible" (Munsell 1969) in describing certain colors. There are dozens of influences on ways in which favorite colors are chosen, but obedience to laws of aesthetics isn't one of them.

A more inclusive term for the force of colors used together is *color effect*. Successful color combinations are realized in terms of goal. Instead of thinking about color groups as harmonious, they can be thought of as successful or unsuccessful. What effect was the colorist trying to achieve in combining the colors? High visibility? Luxury? Color effect encompasses the central issue of color use; in solving the problem at hand, what makes a group of colors work together? Color effects fall into two categories. The first is *color harmony*, the traditional idea of beauty or pleasing quality of colors in combination. The second is *visual impact*, the result of color choices on the visual power of a design or image.

Color Harmony: The Historical Context

Color-order systems were the first concern of the early color theorists because they established a structured field in which to search for laws of color harmony. Balance and order were thought to be so central to color harmony that hues and other qualities of color were frequently associated with rigid laws, numbers, or geometric forms. With his structured charts, Munsell could say that "... every point (color) has its defined number," so that "There can be no new color discovered for which a place and a symbol is not waiting" (Munsell 1969, 10) and conclude that "What we call harmonious color is really balance" (Munsell 1969, 14).

Johannes Itten said that "The concept of color harmony should be removed from the realm of subjective attitude into that of objective principle" (Itten 1961, 19); Goethe repeatedly characterized color harmony as balance (Goethe 1971); and Ostwald referred to "this basic law—Harmony = Order" (Ostwald 1969, 65). There was a complete concurrence of opinion. Balance and order were to be the rule for harmonious colors.

In addition to the obsession with order, early theorists added moral injunctions to laws for color. "People of refinement have a disinclination to colors," Goethe declared firmly (Goethe 1971, 261). Associations of color with chastity, honesty, and social acceptability were common well into the twentieth century. Munsell declared that "Quiet color is a mark of good taste" and "If we wish our children to become well-bred, is it logical to begin by encouraging barbarous [colorful] tastes?" (Munsell 1969, 41).

Two examples are representative of traditional theories of color harmony. Schopenhauer modified Goethe's color circle as a basis for a theory of harmony. His number scale of saturated colors represents the relative light-reflecting value or luminosity of equal size samples of saturated colors. This theory of harmony, which at first seems to concern only hue, is really about complementary hues, value, and relative area. Schopenhauers's number values were

Red	Orange	Yellow	Green	Blue	Violet
6	8	9	6	4	3

(Albers 1963, 43 and Itten 1961, 59).[1]

Each pair of complements added totals 12, or 120 degree arcs of a circle. The three pairs added together total 36, or 360 degrees, a circle in which each *pair* of complements is one of three equal arcs.

Red	6	Orange	8	Yellow	9
Green	6	Blue	4	Violet	3
	12		12		12

. . . .

[1]In *The Art of Color* (1961) and again in the *Elements of Color* (1970) Johannes Itten credits Goethe with this number series for light-reflectance in pure colors. None of the material appears in *Goethe's Color Theory* (1971) and Albers credits Schopenhauer with the creation of this theory, even referring to Goethe's "dismay" at the tampering with his color circle (Albers 1963, 43). It's likely that Albers made the correct attribution.

If the pure colors are imagined as a set of equal, two-inch paper squares, the yellow square (9) is three times as light-reflecting or visible as the violet one (3); the orange (8) is twice as luminous as the blue (4). Red (6) and green (6) are equal.

Because harmony to this generation meant absolute balance or equality, hues in a harmonious grouping had to be equal in light reflectance. To make two-inch squares of pure color harmonious there would have to be three violet squares for each yellow or two blue for each orange. Using this rule for harmony, a shirt with equal width yellow and violet stripes would be disharmonious. Only if the violet stripes were three times as wide as the yellow ones would the shirt would be harmonious!

A second mathematics-based concept of harmony is Johannes Itten's theory of color chords, which illustrate harmonies based on variants of complementary contrast. Itten superimposed geometric forms (squares, rectangles, triangles, hexagons) over the color wheel to demonstrate what he called "Harmonious chords," calling them "Systematic color relationships capable of serving as a basis for composition" (Itten 1961, 72). Although he describes his chords as dyads, triads, tetrads, and hexads, spelling out each group of colors by name, each is a variation of only one idea—complementary contrast.

Color Harmony: A Contemporary View

In the same way that there are too many colors for each to have a name, there are too many possible pleasing ways to combine colors for any rigid set of "laws" to be formulated. Even using a limited definition of color harmony, imagine that 16 million possible computer-generated colors were multiplied into all possible harmonious combinations. The number of possibilities is unimaginable.

In spite of the shift in focus from eighteenth-century philosophical ideal to twentieth-century market appeal, there's an enduring assumption that laws of color harmony really do exist. If the traditional laws of harmony seem flawed and or even ridiculous now, the observations made in determining those laws remain fresh and valid. Buried in the classical ideas of color harmony are paremeters for creating pleasing combinations that transcend historical theories, individual taste, or cultural bias. A colorist can generate an almost endless stream of predictably pleasing, marketable color groupings by working within guidelines that emerge from an idea stated perfectly by Josef Albers: "What counts here—first and last—is not so-called knowledge, but vision—seeing" (Albers 1963, 2). Albers wasn't the first to recognize that visual experience, not conscious choice, controls the perception of colors as harmonious, but he was the first to assert the primacy of the visual experience over intellectual considerations.

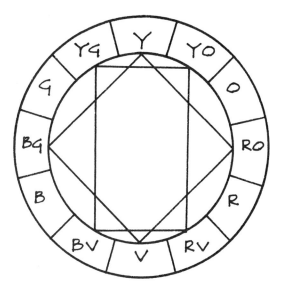

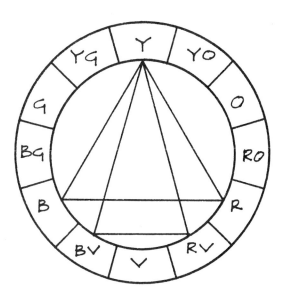

Figure 7–1 *Harmonious Color Chords of Johannes Itten.* Each of these theoretical color harmonies has its basis in complementary contrast.

Intervals and Harmony

The nature of human intelligence has been described as the search for order in all things. Babies demonstrate this without words when they place toy rings on a stick in size order. Adults categorize to control information in the same way—large to small, A to Z, ascending numbers, dates, or sizes. Intervals, particularly even intervals, represent order in perception. Even intervals are easy for the eye to discriminate. Very little effort is needed to discriminate between well-spaced intervals of hue, value, or saturation. The message delivered is steady and uncomplicated. Even intervals don't challenge, disturb, vibrate, or vanish. They are pleasing because they are visually and intellectually comfortable. Intervals between colors are the fill-ins for limited palettes, extending the range of colors without disturbing the overall color composition. The practical applications of this concept extend to all areas of color choice. As an example, a green and red design may call for a dark line. Black is a possibility, but it's visually independent of the color scheme and will give a coloring book type of outline. The mix of red and green, an extremely dark brown, lends a chromatic but still value-contrasting note that has more connection to the red/green palette. A neutral light background for the red and green design can also be a middle mix of the two diluted to a tint. This, too, is more compatible than a random selection of white or off-white.

Hue and Harmony

Color theorists have concentrated ideas of harmony on the relationships between hues. Value as a factor in harmony has been a second consideration—except for Munsell, who stressed the harmony of middle values (Munsell 1969)—and saturation a last consideration. In almost all theories of color harmony, the concern with hue has been further focussed on the complementary relationship. Pure hues are usually acknowledged to be harmonious when used alone or in an analogous grouping. The "menu" of harmonious combinations thus includes single hues, adjacent hues, and opposite hues. The only missing hue combination is that of two primaries. Common sense tells us that two primaries, like blue and yellow or yellow and red, can be used together in pleasing ways. When we add "two primaries" to the list, the menu of possible harmonious hue combinations becomes

Any hues used together can be harmonious.

This doesn't mean that any hues used together *are* harmonious. It means only that there are no inherently bad hue combinations.

The complementary relationship between colors is used so commonly, consistently, and successfully that there must be underlying truth to the idea that complements are harmonious. Red and green, "peach" (orange) and blue, violet and "gold" (yellow) are recurring and complementary combinations. When Goethe called the complements completing colors, he reminded us that complementary pairs contain all three primaries, that the eye seeks equilibrium, and that therefore complementary colors used together fulfill or complete the needs of the eye. Hues in complementary relationship are physiologically satisfying. Again, "What counts here—first and last—is not so-called knowledge, but vision—seeing" (Albers 1963, 2). Not surprisingly, the visual experience supports the classical theories of color harmony. First the eye seeks the complements, then we find them pleasing. Complements used in even intervals please the eye on two levels. The eye is satisfied physiologically because equilibrium is in place and even intervals require little effort to discriminate. Complements in even intervals combine two levels of comfort. Analogous colors are intervals between hues. Analogous hues don't satisfy the eye's need for equilibrium, but they, too, are comfortable to the eye because they make perceptual sense.

Value and Harmony

Hue relationships alone are incomplete ideas about color harmony. Although the major role of value contrast is in creating image, traditional color theory states that

> Even intervals of value are harmonious.
>
> Middle values are harmonious.
>
> Equal values are harmonious.

The most important and useful fact about value is that even intervals of value are harmonious. If the same design is rendered twice, once in even intervals of value and once in uneven ones, the design using even intervals will invariably be preferred. Even intervals don't have to extend from great darks to very light. Even intervals of value are harmonious as long as each step is well-distanced from the others—easy to tell apart and easy to see. Even intervals of value are easy for the eye to discriminate at the same time as they meet the human need for order. Intervals too close to a viewer's threshold are uncomfortable because they're hard to see.[2]

Middle values in any hues have been traditionally considered to be more harmonious than the extremes of light or dark. There's plenty of

. . . .

[2]Intervals too small for the eye to discriminate and which appear to blend are used to create an illusion of shading. This is a use separate from the idea of harmonious intervals of value.

dark-to-light range in the middle values; only the darkest and lightest ends of the scale are excepted. Middle value means hues within a visual comfort range—hues easy to detect. We choose first those colors that we can discriminate with minimum effort.

The greater the contrast in values, the stronger the image and the more stimulating or exciting the effect. A composition limited to the middle range of values, no matter what the ground is or how many hues it has, risks being literally monotonous. With this in mind, the statement "Equal values are harmonious" seems unpromising. With no value contrast there are no value differences to excite the eye. Why, then, are these two value relationships (middle values in any hues and equal values in any hues) traditionally considered harmonious?

To say that "middle values are harmonious" and "equal values are harmonious" is to state an incomplete truth. The ways in which these colors are used matters a great deal. There are two ways in which hues of close or equal value are used harmoniously. Each depends for its success on the intent of the colorist. First, hues of middle or equal value are successful as carried colors against a contrasting darker or lighter ground. The resulting image emerges from the ground with a relatively flat but richly colored effect.

A second way in which hues of close or equal value are used with great success is when no image is intended. Hues of close or equal value used together without a contrasting ground create complex surfaces without image or pattern. Some of the most beautiful stone and ceramic products, papers, textiles, and wall finishes depend on an interplay of different hues in close value. Most often the hues are analogous, but they can be quite different as long as the values are close. These broken color surfaces are more like optical mixes than anything else. Optical mixes depend on small scale for the eye to fuse several colors into one new one. Larger patches or areas of color that are close in value will also meld into a richly embellished surface to be used alone or as grounds for images or patterns laid over them.

Saturation and Harmony

A good argument can be made for asserting that any muted color is more harmonious than a more saturated one. In the presence of muted colors the eye is at rest. But color harmony is not about the restful or stimulating qualities of single brilliant or muted colors. It refers to collective impression, not single qualities. Color compositions are most successful when the level of saturation is relatively constant. Brilliant designs are exciting and muted ones are restful, but neither is naturally more harmonious than the other. When a general level of saturation is established, any atypical element disrupts the composition. One pure color inserted into a palette of muted ones will pop forward and dominate. It doesn't "belong" to the whole. The muted colors will appear gray, dirty, and receding by contrast. A single muted element inserted into a composition of pure colors will be a blot in the clean, bright colors around it.[3]

Intervals of saturation between a pure color and gray are sometimes used by illustrators to indicate roundness without great depth. The most familiar way to indicate roundness in two-dimensional forms is to shade them with dark, which recedes sharply, and highlight them with light, which appears to advance. Because more brilliant colors appear to advance and muted ones to recede, using intervals of saturation instead of value also creates a three-dimensional illusion in a softer, less dramatic way. The absence of dark and light keeps the image closer to the surface—less "near and far." In a floral printed fabric, for example, intervals of saturation from bright green to muted gray-green may be used to suggest leaves receding into gentle shadow. Roses may be illustrated in intervals from brilliant pink to pinkish gray or from yellow to gray. Complicated textiles like Aubusson carpets have dozens of hues, each in many steps of saturation as well as many steps of value. Using intervals of saturation to illustrate depth or dimension in this way doesn't make brighter colors "pop" out of a composition. Steps from bright hue to gray make sense to the eye. The saturation level of this kind of composition is a balance between the vivid and muted elements. Colors composed together in this way work together, not individually, to establish a cumulative, overall level of saturation.

Simple and Complex Harmonies

There's no way to disregard the evidence that a great deal of what we find harmonious is dictated not by conscious choice, but by the involuntary responses of our eyes and minds. Color choices are affected by the need for equilibrium, the comfort level of vision, and logic in perception. We have a built-in bias toward certain combinations. What the eye sees is fundamental. It's disconcerting to think that color preferences are made unconsciously. Happily, it isn't that simple. The eyes dictate boundaries of comfort, but designers insert conscious choice into all things. That's what makes design, and that's what makes them designers.

Simple compositions have only one or two colors against a ground. Other compositions may have literally hundreds of colors. Some elaborate combinations are glorious; others are a mess. An elaborate composition is the sum of its parts. Each hue in a design may have any number of sequences of analogy, value, or saturation. Before any other consideration, the intervals of these individual elements must be well spaced.

. . . .

[3]In artwork and illustration, brilliant tints or highly saturated colors are used in muted compositions to create areas of emphasis. Inserting one or two brilliant colors in a muted composition generates high visibility for those colors and separates those colors from the composition as a whole.

Extending the guidelines for simple color harmonies into more complex ones calls for two additional observations.

Successful complex color compositions have a major or dominant hue, often in an analogous grouping. They may also have a minor, supporting one.

A carpet may have dozens or yarns within an analogous blue/green range. Some may be brilliant; others grayed to indicate shading. Some may be dark, others may be light. The blues and greens together are the major theme; the dominant hue is blue-green. Small quantities of red or red-orange added to the composition create a foil for the blue-greenness. The warm colors support and reinforce the cool ones, emphasizing the impact of blue-greenness. Most often the reinforcing, minor role is played by a complement or near-complement of the major hue. Designs in which two or more hue families compete for equal attention are generally less successful than those with major/minor hue relationships.[4]

A recurring problem in design is creating a harmonious visual link between two or more apparently incompatible colors. You need a sofa and have no money; you have inherited Aunt Maude's buttercup yellow sofa but it will have to sit on your dusty rose rug.

Even intervals or steps between colors, no matter what their characteristics of hue, value, and saturation, will produce a harmonious grouping.

The resulting sequence of colors still has to play by the rules. It may be that the group must be used as carried colors against a darker or light ground. But no matter how unlikely and incompatible two colors may seem at first, a series of intervals between them will establish a kind of order that the eye will accept as harmonious and that can be used to create a successful color composition.

Visual Impact

Graphic quality means the "readability" of a composition. Only value contrast creates graphic image. This visual power requires no hue. Black and white create the most contrasting and therefore the most powerful images. A second kind of visual power is the high-impact, shock-value quality of certain hues. These hues demand the eye's immediate attention. Saturated hues are stimulating to the eye, but not all

. . . .

[4]This statement is in direct opposition to the idea that perfect balance of the complements is the perfect harmony.

saturated hues have high impact. Pure violet is too dark to compete for attention with many other colors; when violet is used for high impact it's used as a tint. High-impact colors are both hue-intense and light-reflecting. Strong tints of red-violet or saturated yellow-green, for example, are high impact colors. All "Dayglo" colors, which contain a special light-reflecting component in the medium, have high impact. High-impact colors are also used, symbolically, to warn. The Occupational Safety and Health Administration (OSHA) has precisely specified paint colors for specific hazards—a violet for radiation, a red for fire equipment, a yellow for school buses, and so on. OSHA colors are specified by law. School bus yellow is just what Congress has decreed it to be. High-impact colors contrast strongly with the natural environment. Red fire engines are so visible because they combine high visibility and a strong contrast to landscape or streetscape colors. Shock-value colors and combinations may or may not be graphically "readable." That remains a function of value contrast. Extremely brilliant colors are likely to vibrate as well, which makes them poor candidates for readability. The intent and effect of high-impact colors is to draw fast, short-term attention.

Visual Impact and Area

The size of a block of color is less important than its visual impact. Some qualities of color will dominate others even when there is a tiny bit of one and an enormous amount of the other. If the walls, floor, and seats of Madison Square Garden are carpeted with gray carpet and a bright red chair is placed in the center, the chair (tiny area) will be more visually compelling than the carpet (enormous area). The area, or extent of a color, has less importance in visual impact than other qualities of color. Regardless of the area covered, colors will be perceived according to the guidelines of spatial effects. All other factors being equal, a small area of warm color will dominate a larger area of cool color, light color will dominate a larger area of dark, and more saturated or brilliant colors will dominate muted ones. Of course, combinations of colors in which "all factors are equal" except one hardly ever occur. Again it is the dominant quality of a sample—its warmth, high value, or brilliance relative to another color—that will overcome the fact that there is less of it in catching the eye.

Visual Impact and Dissonance

It's fair to say (as an intellectual argument, anyway) that no color combinations are inherently unpleasing. Somewhere, sometime, someone will love a lipstick-red, pea-soup green, gray-violet, and school-bus-yellow dress. On the other hand, it's unlikely that many dresses in this combination will be sold. Most people would find the colors dissonant.

Using dissonant colors is another way to attract attention. Dissonant colorways disturb the eye. They may startle or repel, but they never bore. You may not love the lipstick-red, pea-soup-green, gray-violet, and school-bus-yellow dress, but you won't miss it and you won't forget it. (See Figure C–24.)

References

Albers, Josef. 1963. *Interaction of Color*. New Haven, Connecticut: Yale University Press.

Goethe, Johann von Wolfgang. 1971. *Goethe's Color Theory*. Translated by Rupprecht Matthei. New York: Van Nostrand Reinhold.

Itten, Johannes. 1961. *The Art of Color*. Translated by Ernst Van Haagen. New York: Van Nostrand Reinhold.

Itten, Johannes. 1970. *The Elements of Color*. Edited by Faber Birren. Translated by Ernst Van Haagen. New York: Van Nostrand Reinhold.

Munsell, Albert Henry. 1969. *A Grammar of Colors*. New York: Van Nostrand Reinhold.

Ostwald, Wilhelm. 1969. *The Color Primer*. New York: Van Nostrand Reinhold.

Chapter 8

Color in the Marketplace

Aspects of Color / Color as Style / Period Colors / Time, Place, and Color

Aspects of Color

Color is a powerful tool for designers—a complicated visual language. Besides its importance in design sales, it has a multitude of everyday uses.

Color identifies. It provides instant discrimination between objects of identical form and size—a red file holds the unpaid bills; a green file the paid ones. Color is associative. The most ordinary items of everyday life are identified by color associations. When Mary asks John to look something up in the yellow pages, there's no need to ask where the pages are.

Color is impressional. An abstract composition of blurred blues and greens would never make sense entitled "Desert Scene." Moonscape colors would never be mistaken for Monet's garden.

Color is symbolic, related to cultural experience. Brides wear white in western Europe and red in India. We mourn in black in the West. In India, mourners wear white. In ancient China, the emperor alone wore yellow. The word for red in Old Russian language is synonymous with the word for beautiful. Catholic priests wear black, cardinals red-violet, and the Pope white. Tibetan lamas wear robes of brilliant yellow.

Color affects all of our senses, many times in ways not fully understood. A blue room seems cool at 65 degrees, a pink room feels warm at the same temperature. There are studies of the relationship of color perception to music, mathematics, mood, healing, taste, and the sense of touch.

Color is stimulating, calming, expressive, disturbing, impressional, cultural, and associative. It pervades every aspect of our visual lives. Most of all, color is enriching. It embellishes the ordinary and gives beauty and drama to everyday objects. If black and white images bring us the news of the day, color writes the poetry.

Color as Style

There will always be skirts, but hemlines change as often as the weather. Men wore powdered wigs in 1756 and duck-tail haircuts in 1956. Plumpness is beauty in 1890; slenderness is beauty in 1980. Style is about what purchasers want today. Yesterday's style can't be sold. There are styles in color as surely as in hemlines. Today consumer demand for new colors is created a combination of cycles in color taste and by deliberate marketing. The spread of a new color is usually initiated by the apparel industry, trickles down to home furnishings, then to hard goods like appliances and cars. The demand created by color stylists at the top of the pyramid forces obsolescence of older goods. In goods that are mass marketed and have a brief sales life, like clothing, choice of colors can spell life or death to a manufacturer. Survival may mean being able to anticipate, or at least keep up with, current fashion colors. "Color as style" has become so important commercially that industries now research consumer reactions to proposed colorings before going into production on new items. Professional organizations like the Color Association of the United States and the Color Marketing Group exist to provide information and guidance on the next wave of demand. Professional colorists consult on everything from hair color to building exteriors.

Period Colors

Consumers are a complicated crowd—varying by age, sex, income, education, cultural background, and geography. Target markets exist for everything, including target markets for colors. No matter how successful current fashion colors may be, there are consumers at all economic levels who demand products in so-called "traditional" colorings. Particularly in home furnishings, there's a permanent market for goods in what are thought to be "period" colors. There are color palettes typical of specific cultures and historic periods. The fragile tints of 18th-century France, the colors of restored colonial Williamsburg, the traditional batiks of Southeast Asia, and the earth colors of precolonial African textiles are examples of colorings associated with special times and cultures.[1]

"Period" colors haven't always been historically accurate and they're not all accurate today. Many people prefer the muted quality of faded textiles and paints and these muted colors are marketed as traditional colorings. In actual fact, colorants oxidize (change after exposure to air and/or light) over time. Years of accumulated grime mute even the most durable colors and current levels of air pollution accelerate the destructive processes. Not only do colors alter by soiling and oxidizing, the various colors in a composition do so at different rates. In a single textile or painted object, some colors will change enormously over time and others hardly at all so the original balance of colors achieved by the artist or artisan is lost.[2]

Sophisticated techniques of analysis now make it possible for the original colors of paintings, textiles, and decorative objects to be determined with some accuracy. New methods of cleaning uncover close-to-original hues. Textiles and paints are now available (called documents or documentary colors) as facsimiles of the antique ones as they were when they were new and not in their faded states. (See Figure C–22.)

. . . .

[1] A wonderful general source for historic color information is *The Color Compendium* by Hope and Walch, published by Van Nostrand Reinhold in 1990.

[2] A few ancient colorings survive nearly intact. The tomb paintings of the Egyptians, rendered in durable earth pigments, were protected for thousands of years by the dry air of the desert and protected sites of the tombs. Many medieval illuminated manuscripts survive in astonishingly beautiful condition in part because of the durability of the colorants and in part because they were protected as religious objects.

The new restoration and research techniques have caused a small revolution in historic preservation. Building restoration, both interior and exterior, has taken on a new and controversial face as color accuracy supersedes the old conventions. When the "Rose Room" in the White House was refurbished during the Kennedy administration, there was a furor over the brilliant red-violet walls. The restored color was as it had been originally, but it wasn't expected by a public used to thinking of "period" colors as subdued.

Restored colors of antique art and decoration do reflect the taste of a period, but to a greater extent they reflect the colorants available in that place and time.[3] The technical limitations of palette which dictated colors of the past no longer exist. Modern chemistry produces an almost limitless range of colors in every imaginable medium. Resistance to oxidation remains a problem and soil, particularly airborne soil and pollutants, is probably more of a problem than ever before.

Time, Place, and Color

International communication has blurred the lines of what once were colorings typical of different cultures. Classical Japanese combinations are as common in Milan as in Tokyo. The batiks of Southeast Asia compete with the ruanas of Peru and the pottery of ancient China as sources of colorings for all uses. There have never been richer or more varied sources of inspiration available to colorists. In the free-wheeling climate of twentieth-century design, any combination is welcome, any combination can be beautiful.

Professional colorists are blessed with a multitude of sources, but they're also faced with conflicting demands. Market-appeal of colors is crucial to sales and therefore to the design process. To compete in the marketplace, colorists must provide manufacturers with innovative colorings, current fashion colors, and classic, timeless colorings of equal marketability.

Style, psychology, and fashion trends are independent of the visual experience. *Understanding Color* addresses the visual experience alone. Style is change, but the visual experience is constant. Understanding color means the ability to control color effects. The ability to control color effects means artistic empowerment and a competitive edge in any design industry.

. . . .

[3]Art historians date textiles, pottery, and fine and decorative arts by coloring as well as design. For example, Japanese prints can be dated in part by the presence or absence of the aniline dyes introduced in Japan in the nineteenth century.

Reference

Hope, Augustine and Walch, Margaret. 1990. *The Color Compendium.*
New York: Van Nostrand Reinhold.

Glossary

achromatic Having no discernible hue or color.

additive mixture Color seen as a result of light only.

additive primaries Wavelengths of light that must be present to yield white light. Also, the wavelengths of light that must be present render all colors of objects—red, blue, and green.

afterimage A mirage or false image generated by the eye in response to stimulation by a single color in the absence of its complement.

analogous colors Colors adjacent on the spectrum; sometimes defined as hues limited to the range between a primary and secondary.

artists' spectrum The full range of visible hues as postulated by Goethe: red, orange, yellow, green, blue, and violet; expandable to include any and all hues in between them. A synonym of color wheel.

Bezold Effect An effect in which all colors in a composition appear lighter by the addition of light outline or darker by the addition of dark outline. Or an effect in which a colored ground appears lighter because of a carried linear design in light line or darker because of a carried linear design in dark line.

brilliance The combined qualities of high light reflectance and strong hue, typically found in saturated colors and strong tints.

carried colors Colors in an image or design that are laid on the background. (See *ground*.)

chroma A synonym of hue or color; the name of a color. Also, the relative hue and intensity of a color. (See *hue*.)

chromatic Having hue or color.

color A category of visual experience including hue, value, and saturation. Also a synonym for hue or chroma; the name of a color. (See *hue*.)

colorant A substance that reacts with light by absorbing some wavelengths and reflecting others, giving an object or surface its hue. Also called color agent.

colorway A specific combination of colors for a product—textile, wall covering, or other—available in more than one combination of colors; as "This paisley is available in a red colorway, a green colorway, and a gray colorway."

color wheel A synonym for the artists' spectrum.

complements, complementary colors Colors directly opposite each other on the artists' spectrum or color wheel. Every pair of complements contains the three primary colors—red, yellow, and blue—in some proportion or mixture.

contrast reversal A variation of afterimage in which the "ghost" image is seen as negative of the original image and as its complementary color.

dilution Changing a pure or saturated hue by the addition of black, white, gray, or its complement.

dye (dyestuff) A colorant that is fully dissolved in a vehicle such as water or other liquid; a colorant in solution. Traditionally dyes were organic, but modern colorants are less rigidly categorized.

equilibrium An involuntary, physiological state of rest sought by the eye. Equilibrium occurs when all three (additive or subtractive) primary colors are present within the field of vision.

Fibonacci series A series of intervals starting with 0, 1, in which each step is the sum of the two preceding (0, 1, 1, 2, 3, 5, 8, 13, 21, etc.). Used to characterize some sequences of color intervals.

field In carpet and flag design, the term for the background upon which colors are laid. (See *ground.*)

fugitive Easily fading or deteriorating color, usually used in reference to colorants.

full color See *saturated color.*

gloss A highly polished, light-reflective surface quality.

ground The background against which colors are seen or laid.

harmony The pleasing joint effect of two or more colors.

hue The name of the color: red, orange, yellow, green, blue, and violet. Synonyms are chroma or color.

hue intensity The saturation or purity of a color, its vivid versus dull quality. (See *saturation.*)

illuminant mode of vision Color seen as light; viewer and light source only.

incident beam The beam of light emitted by a light source.

intensity Sometimes used as a synonym for chroma or saturation, the strength of a hue. (See *hue intensity* and *light intensity.*)

interval A visual step between color samples. Even intervals are visually equidistant steps between colors.

lamp The correct term for a light bulb.

light Visible energy.

light intensity The light-reflecting quality of a color. (See *luminosity* and *value*.)

luminosity Literally, light emitted without heat. Used to describe the light-reflecting quality of a color. Luminous colors reflect light; nonluminous colors absorb light.

matte A smooth but dull, unpolished surface quality.

maximum chroma The strongest possible manifestation of a hue.

medium A liquid, paste, viscous, solid, or other vehicle (substance) into which pigments or dyes have been introduced to form a transferable colorant such as paint, dye, or crayon.

metameric pair Two objects that appear to match under one set of light conditions but do not match under a different set of light conditions.

metamerism The phenomenon that occurs when two objects which appear to match under one set of light conditions do not match under another set of light conditions.

monochromatic Containing one hue only.

monotone Color without variation. Generally used to describe two or more colors of close or identical value and saturation.

object mode of vision The presence of a light source, object, and a viewer.

optical mix A new color that is seen as a result of the close juxtaposition of small areas of two or more other colors.

palette Literally, a board or plate upon which colors are mixed. Used to describe a group of colors used characteristically by an individual artist or designer or in a specific design, group of designs, or body of work.

pastel An apparel industry term for colors diluted by white to high or middle value; clean tints with little or no muted quality.

physical spectrum The full range of visible colors of light as postulated by Newton: red, orange, yellow, green, blue, indigo (blue-violet), and violet.

pigment A colorant that is finely ground and suspended as minute particles in a vehicle. Traditionally pigments were inorganic (earth colors), but modern chemistry has blurred this definition. Pigments in general are opaque.

primary colors The simplest colors of the artists' spectrum; those that cannot be reduced or broken down into component colors: red, yellow, and blue. (See also *additive primaries,* and *process colors.*)

process colors In printing and other graphic arts media, yellow, cyan (blue-green), and magenta (red-violet) colorants that when mixed or laid over one another result in nearly all possible colors on the printed page. Used with the addition of black in four-color printing.

process primaries Cyan (blue-green), magenta (red-violet), and yellow. (See *process colors.*)

pure color See *saturated color* and *maximum chroma.*

reflected beam The beam of light reaching an object which is reflected back to the eye.

saturated color The most intense manifestation of a color imaginable—the "reddest" red or "bluest" blue. Saturated colors are undiluted by black, white, or gray. Synonyms are pure color, full color, or hues at maximum chroma.

saturation The degree of purity of a color, its hue intensity, or vivid quality as opposed to muted or dull quality. A fully saturated color can contain one or two of the primary colors but never the third. Saturated color does not contain any black, white, or gray.

secondary colors Colors made up of two primary colors: in subtractive mixtures orange (red and yellow), green (blue and yellow), and violet (red and blue); in additive mixtures cyan (blue and green), yellow (red and green), and magenta (blue and red).

shade A pure color mixed with black.

simultaneous contrast A spontaneous color effect resulting from a physiological response of the eye to stimulation by one color only. The eye, seeking equilibrium (presence of all three primaries in the field of vision), generates the missing primary or primaries.

single interval The smallest difference between close samples that a viewer can distinguish; established by the individual's threshold. (See *interval* and *threshold.*)

spectral reflectance curve The characteristic pattern of relative energy emitted by a specific lamp at the various wavelengths.

spectrum The full range of visible hues. (See *artists' spectrum* and *physical spectrum.*)

spreading effect See *Bezold Effect.*

standard A sample against which a color is matched in dyeing.

subtractive mixtures Colors seen as the result of the absorption of light, the colors of objects.

subtractive primaries The primary colors of perceived objects; the artists' primaries: red, yellow, and blue.

tertiary colors Colors made of any mix of the three primaries (or complementary primary and secondary colors); "brown" or chromatic neutrals.

threshold That point in vision at which an individual can just distinguish between two close samples.

tint A pure color plus white.

tone A nonspecific word referring to change in value, light or dark within a hue.

transparence illusion An illusion in which opaque colors are made to appear transparent; done by overlapping two different colors and placing the middle mix of the two in the area of overlap.

value Relative light and dark with or without the presence of hue. High value samples are light; low value samples are dark.

vehicle A liquid, paste, viscous, wax, chalk, or other substance into which pigments, dyes, or other colorants may be introduced to form a medium such as oil paint, textile dye, or crayon.

wavelength A pulse of energy emitted by a light source at specific distances apart. In wavelengths of visible light (visible energy) each wavelength is perceived as a separate color.

The Workbook

General Instructions

Work in natural light whenever possible. Fluorescent light is the least satisfying for color exercises. If natural light isn't available, a combination of incandescent and fluorescent light works well. Art and architectural suppliers sell a clip-on desk lamp with this double light source combination.

Be sure that the working surface is clean and free from old dried pigments, food remnants, oils, or other contaminants. A protective drawing table pad (similar to one used by architects) can be rolled out on any table and provides a good surface. Clean the working surface regularly with any powder or liquid abrasive cleaner and wipe free of grit with clean water.

Rest your eyes frequently when working by alternating exercises or activities. The ability to see differences in colors declines with eye fatigue. Assignments involving saturated hues of equal value are particularly tiring. Plan to do these in several short sittings, not all at once.

Make a "viewing paper" about 3"–4" square for comparing samples. The opening should be about 1"–1 1/2" in diameter.

Resist "naming" the papers or paints. The same piece of paper may be the "answer" to more than one question. Approach each problem separately as if it were the first and only one to be done.

Figure W–1 Make a viewing paper for isolating color samples for comparison. Use any stiff white paper. Cut the paper to approximately 5" × 7". Cut a hole in the center about 1 1/2" in diameter.

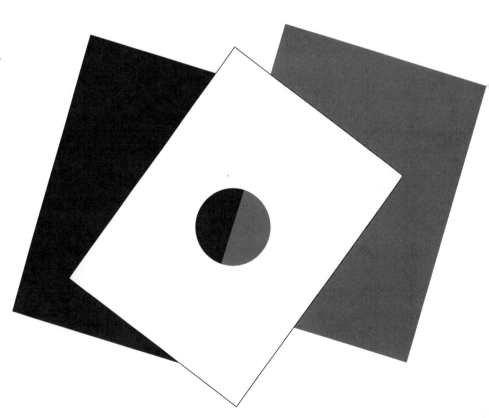

Color Papers

Color papers come in boxed sets made by Color Aid Corporation and other manufacturers. The 6″ × 9″ size is the most useful for classroom work. If any color is used up in class work, single sheets can be purchased individually.

Discard the numbered chart in the box immediately or put it away.

Initial or mark each piece on the back with some identifying mark. Papers are easily mixed up between students in class.

Mixing Gouache Paints

Fill the eyedropper or monoject with clean water for diluting colors. Never let the monoject or eyedropper touch paints or dirty water. Even a drop of paint or dirty water will permanently contaminate it.

Tube colors must be mixed to painting consistency. Use an old brush for mixing. Put about a teaspoonful of tube color or colors onto a mixing tray or into a clean jar; add droplets of clean water until the paint is the consistency of light cream and very smooth.

Colors directly from the tube can be very good saturated colors and will execute the exercises well. Some students prefer the result of a combination of two tube colors. For example, cobalt blue and ultramarine mix well to form an opaque saturated blue. Experiment freely with mixes until you are satisfied, then prepare a small jar of each saturated color needed for the assignment or for the course.

Label each mixed color immediately on the side of the jar, using either a china marker or small stick-on labels and permanent marker (nonpermanent marker will run if it gets wet). Colors that are very different when dry often appear identical when wet. Don't label the cap because caps are easily mixed up.

For tints, mix white to painting consistency, then add hue a bit at a time in tiny quantities. For shades, mix the hue to painting consistency and add tiny amounts of black a bit at a time until the desired color is reached. Always let "test" mixed colors dry completely on the paper before you continue to add white or black.

Dried paints in the container can be remixed perfectly. Add hot water in droplets, allow to stand briefly, and mix to painting consistency.

Brushes

Brushes will vary in performance depending on paper, paint, and area to be covered. Test smaller and larger and round and flat brushes with each color to find the most effective for any particular set of conditions.

Never let brushes rest in water jars or on the bristle end. Clean immediately after use with mild soap and cool water, gently restore to shape, and let dry upright. Hot water will loosen bristles.

Painting

Fill a large container with clean water. Use the water jar only for rinsing brushes, never for diluting paint.

Use one kind of paper for both finished work and for test patches of color. The finished appearance of the same paint mixture may vary from paper to paper.

Paper will absorb the natural skin oils from your hand, causing it to repel the paint. Protect clean paper and finished work by using a piece of clean paper under your working hand. Tracing paper works well for this. The paper will also protect against accidental spills or spattering.

Apply paint once, quickly, and allow to dry completely. Try to avoid a second coat and never "scrub" the paint on.

Some tube colors will separate in the jar after being thinned to painting consistency but will still perform well when stirred thoroughly and applied. Some combinations need constant remixing. Test every mixed color on scrap paper before proceeding.

To compare a new color to one already finished, cut strips of paper about 1″–2″ wide with a utility knife or scissors. Paint a test patch of the new color across the width of the strip and let it dry, then compare it to the completed sample. Don't do test patches on the edges of torn paper. The finished result will be different when painted onto a fresh piece.

Allow each color to dry completely on the paper before applying the one next to it. Wet colors will bleed into one another.

Wet or liquid colors will be very different from dried paint. Always allow samples time to dry completely before making a judgment about the finished effect.

Mistakes

There's really no perfect way to paint over a mistake or a color painted into the wrong area. In an emergency, moisten the painted area gently with a brush dipped in plain water (don't flood it with water) and allow to stand briefly. When the paint has softened, blot once firmly with paper towel. Allow the area to dry thoroughly. Repeat if necessary, then allow to dry completely before applying a new color.

Cutting

Cut color papers or painted ones by marking on the backs in pencil, slightly larger than the desired finished size.

Place the paper face down on the self-healing board. Hold a cork-backed steel ruler firmly over the line to be cut so that the blade is on the pencilled lines. Hold the utility knife vertically and pull firmly and steadily against the steel edge. Change blades every second or third cut, depending on length of the cuts. Blunt blades, not sharp ones, slip and cause injury.

After cutting from the back, turn the paper over and trim from the front only those edges that will be abutted to other papers. Don't trim outside edges yet.

Silk screened and painted papers mark easily so be sure to protect the painted area with scrap paper or tracing paper as you work.

Mounting

Keep rubber cement well thinned. Work in a well-ventilated area when using rubber cement and thinner. Never smoke while using rubber cement or thinner or use either near heat or an open flame.

Spray mount products are not recommended. They require extensive masking and vapors can be dangerous.

Pay close attention to the placement of finished work on the mounting board or sheet. For ordinary mounting (which can be removed) measure the piece to be mounted and mark placement (center or other location) lightly in soft pencil on the mounting board.

Good mounting boards are Bristol paper and illustration board. Fomecore is a lightweight rigid material that can be used as a base for Bristol or illustration board, but it isn't a good surface for direct mounting. Spread thinned rubber cement within the mounting area, allowing it to go slightly over the marked lines. Place the work to be mounted in place on the wet rubber cement. Using scrap paper to protect the work, move and press lightly and quickly until it is in place with adjoining edges placed tightly next to each other but not overlapped. Papers will be slightly uneven at the edges. Allow to dry completely, then clean dried excess cement at the edges with a rubber cement pickup. Try not to rub across your work with the pickup.

Check the vertical and horizontal placements, then use a fresh blade and steel ruler to trim the outside edges of the mounted work. Cut firmly and steadily through the papers, but not through the mounting board (this is easier than it sounds). Don't cut past the edge of the work, the cut will show.

Peel the thin strip of excess color paper off with the point of the utility knife.

For permanent mounting, mark placement lightly with pencil as above, then apply rubber cement to both surfaces. Allow the rubber cement to dry completely on each surface. Place the piece to be mounted exactly in the marked location (one chance only) and using tracing paper to protect the surface of the work, press lightly into place. Allow to dry completely, then clean edges as above.

Copies

More than one copy of a single design can be made by tracing. Draw vertical and horizontal center lines through the design to be copied. These lines are placement guides. Trace the design onto tracing paper, including the two center lines.

Using soft pencil, draw center lines on the new paper. Rub the back of the tracing with very soft pencil. Align the guidelines on the new paper with the guidelines on the tracing. Using hard pencil, draw over the tracing. The soft pencil on the back will rub off onto the paper, leaving a perfect transfer.

Photocopy machines will also accept lightweight watercolor paper if it is cut to the right size.

Protecting Work

Protect the finished, mounted work with tracing paper or other tissue overlay. Mylar or plastic films tend to damage the painted surface and are not recommended.

Labelling—Lettering or Numbering

If lettering or numbering is used, the style, size, and placement should be carefully considered. Uppercase lettering is more effective than uppercase and lowercase. Typed labels that are pasted on are sloppy. Hand lettering in ink and pressure lettering like Letraset are effective.

Repeated Exercises

Because students may do some but not all of the exercises in the workbook, each exercise has been written as if it were alone. Many assignments can be done by extending the work completed in earlier exercises. As you work through the problems, look back to see if you have completed some work that can be a foundation for solving the new one.

Keep your mixed and labelled colors. Remember that dried paints can be remixed perfectly by adding drops of hot water. Mixing paint colors is the most time consuming part of the exercise.

Materials List

1. A minimum number of colors of Winsor and Newton gouache paints is listed below. Students are urged to expand their supplies with additional colors.

Purchase #5 (small) tubes of the following colors. Choices are based on ease of application and low cost. Make sure that tubes are soft. Hard tubes mean that the paint is dried and difficult to use.

Spectrum Yellow

Spectrum Red

Ultramarine

Flame Red

Spectrum Violet

Mistletoe Green

Cyprus Green

Lamp Black

Permanent White (#10 tube)

2. Bristol pad size 9″ × 12″ for mounting finished work. Bristol can also be used as the paper to paint on, but the watercolor paper suggested next gives a better result.

3. Hot press watercolor paper. This is available in large single sheets which can be cut to appropriate sizes.

4. Brushes: Winsor and Newton series #233 or Robert Simmons White Sable; sizes 4 and 6 or student's preference; plus old or cheap brushes for mixing. For serious work, the Winsor and Newton series 7 sable are expensive but wonderful.

5. A drafting table protector or large sheet of inexpensive white paper to use as a clean working surface

6. Roll of 12″ white tracing paper

7. Small covered jars for storing mixed paint. The plastic containers used by take-out restaurants are ideal.

8. Small peel-off labels and a fine-point permanent marker

9. Ceramic or disposable mixing trays

10. Eyedropper or "Monoject 412" water dispenser

11. Container for water, at least 1 quart

12. Cork backed steel ruler

13. Small utility knife and plenty of extra blades

14. Self-healing cutting board, any convenient size

15. Right triangle, at least 8″

16. Compass and protractor

17. Drawing pencils, HB or 2B are recommended

18. Eraser, kneaded or other

19. Rubber cement and thinner, rubber cement pickup

20. Silk screened color paper set: Color-aid® or other, size 6″ × 9″

21. Drafting tape or dots

22. A homemade viewing paper. (See Figure W–1.)

Exercises in Light

1. List as many common light sources as you can. Observe the effect of at least four different light sources on a single red sample of paper or fabric. Describe differences in appearance under the various sources. Repeat using a sample of any other color.

2. Cut two rectangles of stiff cardboard about 2″ × 3″. Select any color wool yarn (no black, gray, or white). Wind the yarn around each cardboard rectangle until the cardboard is covered by thread.

    Leave one rectangle as it is with the flat thread wound around it. Form the thread of the second rectangle into a "pom" by removing the cardboard, tying it firmly in the middle, and shearing the looped ends with scissors.

    Describe the difference in appearance between the flat yarn on the cardboard and the cut ends of the pom. What is the reason for the difference?

3. Select two different materials, like fabric and paint or plastic laminate and carpet, which appear to be the same color. Compare them to each other under fluorescent light, incandescent light, daylight, and halogen light. Describe what you see.

Class Exercise in Color Identification

Each student should select from a silk screened color paper pack the 12 saturated colors of the artists' spectrum. Be sure that the back of each paper has been initialled. Keep the 12 papers selected and return all other papers to the box.

Turn to the person next to you. Using only the two sets of 12 colors already selected, reevaluate the selections and decide together on 12 colors of the spectrum. Put rejected colors back into the box. There is now one new set of 12 spectrum colors selected by a pair of students.

Each pair of students turns to another pair. Using the two reevaluated selections of 12 colors, four students reconsider the choices, conclude which are the best 12 colors for a spectrum, and return rejected colors to the box. Four students have now agreed on one set of 12 spectrum colors.

Repeat until the class has four or five sets of group-selected spectrum colors. Compare the four sets to each other.

Exercises in Hue

1. Illustrate the 12 saturated colors of the artists' spectrum in the following two ways:

    (a) Select the 12 basic saturated colors from a color paper pack and paste up as a strip of squares approximately 1″–3/4″ each.
    (b) Using gouache paint, illustrate the 12 spectrum hues in equal arcs of a "doughnut" circle (with an open center).

2. Select a series of saturated hues in the same hue family, moving from warmer to cooler:

    (a) Starting with saturated red, select two more reds in steps moving cooler.
    (b) Starting with the same red, select two or more reds in steps moving warmer.
    (c) Starting with green or violet, select two more greens or violets in steps moving warmer.
    (d) Starting with green or violet, select two more greens or violets in steps moving cooler.

3. Using color papers, illustrate three analogous groupings, using at least three hues in each grouping.

4. Create a simple outlined "coloring book" type of design on white paper. Make two copies of the design.

    (a) Using paint, select two primaries to fill in your design. You may leave white as the ground. Be sure to cover the lines of your drawing completely so that the color is seen in masses or blocks.
    (b) Repeat the design in exactly the same colors, but add a small element containing the missing primary. The missing primary can be added as the primary or as a secondary. For example, if the first two primaries are red and yellow, blue may be added as blue or as green or violet, either of which contains blue.
    (c) Show the two nearly-identical designs to people outside the class who is not aware of the exercise and ask them which they prefer.

Which was chosen? Why?

5. Obtain a sample of screen printed wallpaper. The more colors (screens) in the paper, the better. Select from the Color-aid pack papers to match, as closely as possible, the colors in the wallpaper.

6. Select a middle-gray color paper. Try to select a gray with as little chromatic undertone as possible. Cut six squares approximately 1″.

   (a) Select red, green, orange, blue, yellow, and violet saturated hues from color paper. Cut a square 2 1/2″–3″ of each. Place the complementary colors next to each other and lay a gray square in the center of each hue.

   Work with one pair of complements at a time. Describe differences, if any, in the appearance of the gray square on each hue.

   (b) Select a random variety of tints, shades, and dull hues. Lay a gray square in the center of each sample and compare its appearance to the same gray on another sample. Describe the results.

7. Select the strongest possible red paint and paint a circle approximately 6″ in diameter in the center of a white paper at least 9″ square or cut one out of red paper and mount in the center of a white paper. Place a small black dot, about 1/8″ in the center of the red circle.

   On a second sheet of white paper of the same size place an 1/8″ black dot in the center.

   Stare at the red circle without blinking as long as possible. Blink once and transfer your eyes to the black dot in the center of the blank white paper. What do you see? Why?

8. Select the strongest possible yellow paint. Paint a geometric design of diamonds (or circles) each about 2″ at the widest point in the center of a sheet of white paper 9″ square. There will be 4 diamonds wide and 4 diamonds high with a slight border of white. The diamonds (or circles) should just touch. Have ready a second sheet of blank white paper the same size.

   Stare at the yellow design without blinking as long as possible. Blink once and transfer your eyes to the blank white paper. What do you see? Why?

Exercises in Value

1. Illustrate value without hue. Select any publication (magazine or newspaper) with black and white photographs. Use as many issues as you need, but don't use two different publications. The paper and printing ink should be the same.

   Cut or tear photographs from the publication into small strips or patches of light and dark grays.

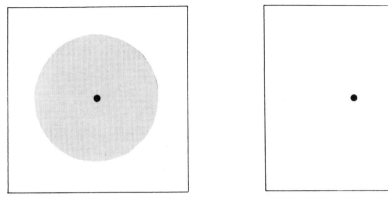

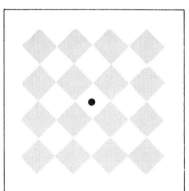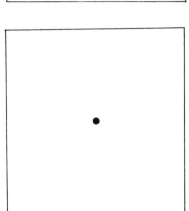

Figure W–2 *Afterimage and Contrast Reversal*. These effects can be demonstrated by creating color cards about 12″ square. Make one with a large red circle; the other with yellow diamonds. Put a black dot into the center of a separate white page. Try each effect separately. Stare at the red circle as long as possible without blinking. Then blink once and look quickly at the white page with the black dot. Repeat the exercise with the yellow diamonds.

Using 9″ × 12″ paper and school paste or rubber cement, arrange the pieces of torn paper into an overlapping collage. Leave none of the white paper visible. Start from the darkest gray and ascend to the lightest one.

Trim the finished collage nearly to approximately 7″ × 10″ and mount onto 9″ × 12″ Bristol paper.

Which sections of the collage were the most difficult to do?

2. Illustrate even intervals of value three ways: in achromatic, warm, and cool colors.

   (a) Paint an achromatic series of nine even intervals of value from lightest gray to near-black.
   (b) Paint a series of nine even intervals of value in blue, green, or violet. Start with the lightest possible tint and end with the darkest possible shade.
   (c) Paint a series of nine even intervals of value in yellow or orange. Start with the lightest possible tint and end with the darkest possible shade.

Which part of the assignment was the most difficult to do?

3. Select one of the following pairs of saturated colors:

Blue and orange

Green and orange

Red and blue

Using color paper, select four intervals of value in the first color of the selected pair. Be sure to stay within one hue and try to keep the intervals as even as possible. Use saturated colors, tints, and shades.

Select four intervals of the second color equal in value to the first four. Paste up as shown below.

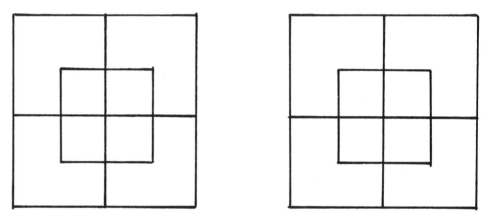

Figure W–3 Start with the lightest of the larger squares of cool hue and arrange clockwise, starting top left. Place the smaller squares of the warm hues in the center also starting with the lightest and working clockwise from top left. Repeat using the warm hues as the larger squares and the cool hues as the smaller ones.

What was the most difficult part of this assignment?

4. Create a simple outlined "coloring book" type of design on white paper. Make two copies of the design.

    (a) Using gouache, mix four grays in well-spaced, even intervals of value. Fill in your design on the white paper. The painted areas should be blocks. Be sure to cover all lines completely. Leave the ground white.

    (b) Using the same four grays, repeat your design, but place the values differently within it.

What happens?

5. Create a simple outlined "coloring book" type of design on white paper. Make four copies of the design.

(a) Using gouache paint, mix four grays in well-spaced, even intervals of value. Fill in your design on the white paper. The painted areas should be blocks. Be sure to cover all lines completely.

(b) Using gouache paint, mix four values of a single hue (red, red-orange, or orange) equal in value to the grays. Placing the colors in the same value relationships as the grays, paint the design in the warm color.

(c) Using gouache paint, mix four values of a single hue (blue, green, or violet) equal in value to the grays. Placing the colors in the same value relationships as the grays, paint the design in the cool color.

(d) Select at least three different hues. Using gouache paint, mix a single hue that is equal in value to each of the grays. For example, saturated yellow might be equal to the lightest gray, a tint of blue to the second gray, a tint of blue-violet to the third gray, and so forth.

Placing the colors in the same value relationships as the gray, paint the design in the multicolor combination.

6. Using squares or triangles of color paper, illustrate vanishing boundaries.

7. Using color papers and simple blocks or squares, demonstrate the most extreme example you can of vibration.

8. Using gouache, illustrate a chart of six hues in intervals of equal value. Red, orange, yellow, green, blue, and violet are arranged vertically in five, seven, or nine intervals of value from near-white to near-black.

When the completed chart is read vertically, each of the six hues is illustrated in equal intervals of value.

When the completed chart is read horizontally, the six hues are of equal value.

Helpful hints: Establish a comfortable working size for the painted colors, usually between 3/4"–1/2". Squares or rectangles are equally effective.

Using the ruler and triangle or other drafting equipment, lay out a grid of squares or rectangles. The finished chart must have no spaces between the colors. Using a soft pencil, label your colors R/O/Y/G/B/V and number your steps 1 through 5, 7, or 9 outside the grid.

Select any color and mix a series of value intervals until you are satisfied that the series extends from the lightest tint to the darkest shade in even intervals. Let's assume that the first value scale painted is the yellow. The yellow will be the standard for the chart. Each of the other five hues will be compared to it.

Now mix a small jar of each of the other five saturated colors to painting consistency. Work with one hue at a time.

Select the second saturated color—red, for example. Compare the red to the steps on the yellow scale. Saturated red may be equal in value to a step on the yellow scale or it may not. If red is not equal in value to any step on the yellow scale, the red will not appear on the chart as a pure color. It will appear on the chart only in tints and shades.

Repeat until all six hues are painted.

Exercises in Saturation

1. Using Color-aid paper, select the saturated colors red, orange, yellow, green, blue, and violet.

   Select a gray equal in value to each hue.

   Find the middle interval between each pure color and its gray of equal value. Cut the hue, the gray, and the middle interval into squares about 1″ and mount in a strip.

   Describe the hue, value, and saturation of the middle intervals.

2. Select the three complementary pairs from the color paper pack.

   Select three even intervals between each pair (total of five steps, including the pure hues). Cut each color into a square approximately 1″. With the complements at each end, paste up each pair illustrating the sequence from one complement to the other.

   What is characteristic of the first step next to each pure color? Describe it in terms of hue, value, and saturation.

   What is characteristic of the middle intervals?

3. Create a simple outlined "coloring book" type of design on white paper. Make four copies of the design.

   Using gouache paint, select any pair of complements. Use only these two hues and white to make the four identical designs appear as different as possible from each other. Use the colors as pure colors, tints, or mixed in any way at all, but use only the two complements and white.

4. Create a simple outlined "coloring book" type of design on white paper. Make two copies of the design.

   (a) Paint the design in any saturated colors and/or tints.
   (b) Using exactly the same hues and values, repeat in muted colors.

Exercises in Illusion

1. Using color paper, make one saturated hue or tint appear to be two different hues by placement on different grounds.

2. Using color paper, make one saturated hue or tint appear to be two different values by placement on different grounds.

3. Using color paper, make a muted hue appear more and less muted by placement on different grounds.

4. Using color paper, make a tertiary color appear as two completely different colors by placement on different grounds.

5. Using color paper, make any two different colors appear to be the same color by placement on different grounds.

6. Create an illusion of fluting with gouache paint or color paper.

7. Using color paper, demonstrate transparence illusions:

   (a) in grays only
   (b) using one hue in two different values
   (c) using two different pure hues or tints
   (d) using a pure hue or tint and any gray
   (e) using one warm and one cool hue, in any values or levels of saturation

In each case, which color appears to be on top? Explain.

8. Using gouache paint, create an illusion of texture using:

   (a) black, gray, and white only
   (b) analogous colors
   (c) complementary colors

Describe the differences in your results.

9. Using color paper cutouts or gouache paints, demonstrate spreading effect (Bezold Effect).

Exercises in Harmony

1. Create a simple outlined "coloring book" type of design on white paper. Make three copies of the design.

   Using gouache paint, mix a generous quantity of any four or more saturated colors. They may be primaries, secondaries, analogous colors, or any combination of saturated hues. This is the "base" set of colors for this exercise.

   Using the pure colors you have mixed, make a second set of the same, but mute each by adding some of its complement. Add white to the muted hues so that the values are the same as the original, saturated set of colors.

(a) Paint two versions of your design, first entirely in the pure colors, then entirely in the muted ones. Keep the placement of colors identical.

(b) Paint the muted colorway again, substituting a single pure color for its muted counterpart.

Which designs are more pleasing?

2. Create a simple outlined "coloring book" type of design on white paper. Make two copies of the design.

   (a) Using a gray scale of 9 steps from near-white to near-black, above, paint in your design using steps 2, 5, and 8. Be sure to cover all lines completely. The painted areas should be blocks.

   (b) Using the same gray scale, paint in your design using steps 2, 3, and 7. Make sure that the light to dark relationship is the same— step 2 is in the same area, step 3 replaces 5, step 7 replaces 8.

   (c) Show the two nearly-identical designs to people outside the class who is not aware of the exercise and ask them which they prefer.

3. Create a simple outlined "coloring book" type of design on white paper. Make two copies of the design.

   (a) Select a pair of complementary hues. Mix a color grouping using only those two hues, each in *any levels of value*. The level of saturation should be approximately the same. Paint your design covering 75 percent or more of the area with one hue and the remaining area with the complement.

   (b) Repeat the exercise, using the complements in equal areas.

   (c) Show the two nearly-identical designs to people outside the class who is not aware of the exercise and ask them which they prefer.

Explain your results.

Just for Fun

1. Using block letters either drawn or from a template, and any medium, reinforce the idea of a word using color. Some possible choices are:

   VANISHING

   RAZZLE DAZZLE

   CHAMELEON

   ICE PALACE

   SUNSET

   CONVEX (or CONCAVE)

2. Using any paint in "pointillist" technique (dots of color so tiny that they form an optical mix) and only saturated colors, illustrate any rounded form like an apple or pear.

3. Create a simple outlined "coloring book" type of design on white paper. Make three copies of the design.

    Using gouache paint, illustrate the design in complementary colors as it would appear using Schopenhauer's harmonious proportions.

4. Create a transparence illusion using one warm and one cool color. Manipulate the intervals so that the cool color appears to be on top. Do the assignment again so that the warm color appears to be on top.

Bibliography

Albers, Josef. 1963. *Interaction of Color.* New Haven, Connecticut: Yale University Press.

Billmeyer, Fred W. and Max Salzman. 1966. *Principles of Color Technology.* New York: Interscience Publishers (division of John Wiley & Sons).

Birren, Faber. 1987. *Principles of Color.* West Chester, Pennsylvania: Schiffer Publishing Company.

Chevreul, Michel Eugene. 1967. *The Principles of Harmony and Contrast of Colors and Their Applications to the Arts.* New York: Van Nostrand Reinhold Publishing Company.

The Color Theories of Goethe and Newton in the Light of Modern Physics. Lecture held in Budapest on April 28, 1941 at the Hungarian Club of Spiritual Cooperation. Published in German in May, 1941 in the periodical "Geist der Zeit." English translation courtesy of Dr. Ivan Bodis-Wollner, Rockefeller University, New York, 1985.

Designer's Guide to Color, Volumes I and II. 1984. Translated by James Stockton. San Francisco, California: Chronicle Books.

Eiseman, Leatrice. 1990. *The PANTONE Book of Color.* New York: Harry N. Abrams, Publishers.

Evans, Ralph M. 1948. *An Introduction to Color.* New York: John Wiley & Sons.

Goethe, Johann von Wolfgang. 1971. *Goethe's Color Theory.* Translated by Rupprecht Matthei. New York: Van Nostrand Reinhold.

Goldstein, E. Bruce. 1984. *Sensation and Perception.* Belmont, California: Wadsworth Publishing Company.

Hope, Augustine and Margaret Walch. 1990. *The Color Compendium.* New York: Van Nostrand Reinhold.

Itten, Johannes. 1961. *The Art of Color.* Translated by Ernst Van Haagen. New York: Van Nostrand Reinhold.

Itten, Johannes. 1970. *The Elements of Color.* Edited by Faber Birren. Translated by Ernst Van Haagen. New York: Van Nostrand Reinhold.

Lambert, Patricia. 1991. *Controlling Color*. New York: Design Press.

Light and Color. 1978. General Electric Publication TP-119.

Lighting Application Bulletin. Undated. General Electric publication #205-41311.

Mayer, Ralph. 1981. *The Artist's Handbook of Materials and Techniques*. New York: The Viking Press.

Munsell, Albert Henry. 1969. *A Grammar of Colors*. New York: Van Nostrand Reinhold.

Nicolson, Marjorie Hope. 1966. *Newton Demands the Muse*. Princeton, New Jersey: Princeton University Press.

Ostwald, Wilhelm. 1969. *The Color Primer*. New York: Van Nostrand Reinhold.

Pocket Pal. 1988. Editor Michael Bruno. Memphis, Tennessee: International Paper.

The Random House Dictionary of the English Language. 1967. Editor in Chief Jess Stein. New York: Random House, Inc.

Sargent, Walter. 1964. *The Enjoyment and Use of Color*. New York: Dover Publications, Inc.

Sloane, Patricia. 1989. *The Visual Nature of Color*. New York: Design Press.

Walch, Margaret. 1979. *Color Source Book*. New York: Scribner.

Index

Intervals, 21–23
    even, 22, 23, 64
    Goethe and, 35
    harmony and, 96
    parent-descendent color mixtures and, 21–23
    saturation and, 71–72, 99
    series, 23
    single, 21
    uneven, 22, 23
    value and, 64
Itten, Johannes, 38, 82, 92–94

L

Lamp
    A-lamp, 5
    choice, 7, 11, 12, 16
    color comparison of, 5
    color rendition of objects by, 11
    defined, 5–6
    fluorescent, 5, 11, 12
    full-spectrum, 6
    general light source, 5, 10
    human comfort and performance, 7
    incandescent, 5, 12
    neon, 4, 5
    quantity of light emitted by, 5
    sodium, 5
    spectral reflectance curve of, 5
    see also light, light source
Le Blon, J.C., 33, 34
Light
    absorption of, 7
    defined, 3
    human eye sensitivity to, 6
    incident beam, 8, 9
    indirect, 13–15
    infrared, 3
    modification of, by materials, 7
    primary colors of, 4
    reflected beam, 8, 9
    reflection of, 7–9
    scattering, *see* Light, reflection of

secondary colors of, 4
sources and color rendition of objects, 11
spectrum of visible, 3, 36
surface and, 9–10
transmission of, 7, 8
ultraviolet, 3
visible wavelengths of, 3
white, 4–6
see also Lamp, Light source
Light bulb, 5
Lighting level (quantity of light), 5
Light intensity, *see* Value
Light source, 2–6
    see also Light, Lamp
Line, 77, 89
Luminaire, 5
Luminosity, 13, 66, 93

M

Macbeth lamp, 12
Mass, 77
Matching, 16–17
Materials, modification of light by, 7
Matte surface, 9
Media, 44–48, 53
Medium, 44
Memory color, 26
Metamerism, 16
Mixing affinity, 45
Monochromatic, 51, 69
Morality and color, 34, 37, 93
Munsell, Albert, 37, 39, 92–93

N

Names of colors, 23–25, 40, 51
Nature, 72
Negative space, 77
Neon lamp, 4, 5
Newton, Isaac, 33–35, 39